Hillbilly Gothic

A Memoir of Madness and Motherhood

Adrienne Martini

WITHDRAWN

Free Press

New York
London
Toronto
Sydney

_f_P
FREE PRESS
A Division of Simon & Schuster, Inc.
1230 Avenue of the Americas
New York, NY 10020

For information regarding special discounts for bulk purchases, please
contact Simon & Schuster Special Sales at 1-800-456-6798 or
business@simonandschuster.com.

Designed by Karolina Harris

Manufactured in the United States of America

2   4   6   8   10   9   7   5   3   1

The Library of Congress has cataloged this edition as follows:
Martini, Adrienne.
Hillbilly gothic: a memoir of madness and motherhood / Adrienne Martini.
p. cm.
1. Martini, Adrienne—Mental health. 2. Postpartum depression—Patients—
United States—Biography.
I. Title
RG852 .M36 2006
362.198'760092 B—dc22
2006042512

ISBN-13: 978-0-7432-7273-5
ISBN-10: 0-7432-7273-0

For Maddy

"Left my home in the valley
put the mountains to my back
there's nothing wrong with where I come from
sometimes it's meant to be just that."

—SCOTT MILLER, *Cross the Line*

"As for me, I've chosen to follow a simple course:
Come clean. And wherever possible, live your life
in a way that won't leave you tempted to lie. Fail-
ing that, I'd rather be disliked for who I truly am
than loved for who I am not. So I tell my story. I
write it down. I even publish it. Sometimes this
is a humbling experience. Sometimes it's embarrassing. But I haul around no terrible secrets."

—JOYCE MAYNARD, "For Writers: Writing for Health"

Hillbilly
Gothic

My family has a grand tradition. After a woman gives birth, she goes mad. I thought that I would be the one to escape. Given my spectacular failure, my hope is now that my daughter will be the one.

On the day that I admit defeat, I have been crying for days and I am on my way to the emergency room of my local hospital. But of course since I'm running on empty psychologically, my car would be, too. So I pull into a gas station in the middle of the mother of all summer storms.

No one at the gas station will look at me, which is odd considering that most people will at least give you a smile at any time of day in Knoxville, Tennessee. The July air is heavy and wet. Oily splotches and knots of old gum dot the rain-slicked asphalt. My blue tie-dyed T-shirt is soaked and clinging to my quasideflated postpartum belly, showing all of the other drivers that I am wearing maternity shorts, the kind with the stretchy nylon panel in the front—all that I could fit into two weeks after my daughter's birth. I could have braided the hair on my legs and the hair on my head looked like a nest of live eels writhing in the rain.

My sneakers squoosh as I fumble out my debit card

and swipe it in the pump. Miraculously, my hands remain steady for the first time in a few days, but I sniff and snort constantly as tears pour typhoonlike out of my eyes.

Three other drivers gas up and studiously ignore me, including one right next to me. While Knoxville is known for its general friendliness, I've also discovered that it loves a good spectacle. If a stranger appears to be on the verge of a colorful collapse, gawkers flock for front-row seats. I'd assumed that no one could tell that I'd been crying, what with the rain. I'm lying to myself. My eyes are red-rimmed after forty-eight hours of not sleeping. I'm cursed with a near-constant sorrow so deep that it would make a great bluegrass song. Ralph Stanley and I could make millions, provided I can get through the next twenty-four hours without killing myself.

I'd also assumed that no one would care at this particular station, simply because it is in one of Knoxville's few dicey areas. The projects, such as they are in this small southern city wrapped in Appalachia's arms, are just across the street. The rescue ministry is a few blocks away and, from here, I could toss my car keys into Knoxville's largest nightlife hub, where bars and dance clubs spill out their 2 a.m. drunks, then said drunks wander up to this gas station to stock up on cigarettes and six-packs. The clerks here must have strong nerves or they are researching sociology dissertations.

Still, in the harsh light of day, I am enough of a sight that I unnerve even those who spend their nights dealing with drug-induced shootings and drive-by vomitings. Normally, I'd be proud of this. I always revel in the chance to break out of my cardigan-sweatered shell in a town full of supersized Baptist churches and Junior Leaguers. Now, I look like a freak who scares all of the other freaks. My father would be so proud.

Once gassed up, I'll drive myself to the emergency room, where I'll check myself in to Tower 4, a local psych ward. I could have seen it from my gas pump if it weren't so overcast. I'll stay there for the better part of a week, bonding with my fellow loonies while someone else takes care of my brand-new baby because I am a failure. New moms are supposed to be joy made flesh, yet motherhood and I met like a brick meets water. I'm drowning here, not waving.

This wasn't supposed to happen and, yet, it was inevitable, given my past.

During my colorful confinement, in a conversation with a ward social worker, I described the hillbilly Gothic patchwork of suicides, manic depression, and bipolar disorders that is my mother's family and the notable suicide attempt on my father's side. She commented that it was a wonder I hadn't been there before. Now, I can chuckle when I say that. Then, her astute comment touched off yet another deluge of tears.

I wasn't the first of my generation to log some time in the loony bin. One of my cousins, in her early twenties at the time, was committed after the birth of her first child and was later diagnosed as bipolar. Her older sister has battled depression since her first child was born when she was fresh out of her teens. While most of the madness comes on postpartum, it isn't confined to it. One of her children, who is still a teenager, has also checked in to her local Tower 4, a move that has become my family's version of summering in the Hamptons.

Our tale begins in Parkersburg, West Virginia, a microdot of a town buried in the hollers of the Appalachians. Driving into this part of the country is an adventure to the uninitiated. The road cuts through the mountains, creating a narrow canyon fenced on each side by rock or steep cliffs. Greenery sprouts impossibly from these stark faces. One must pay close attention when arriving in Parkersburg. The unobservant—a person folding a map, say—will miss the downtown and wonder why there are houses in such a desolate area.

Isolation has long been the hallmark of Applachia. Before the era of reliable transportation, entire generations could be born, live, and die without ever clapping eyes on a stranger's face. Even after the rise of Toyotas and cable TV, a deep suspicion of new faces and, to a large extent, new ideas still thrives. This wariness is warranted; rarely is a person from Appalachia portrayed in a flattering light. An Appalachian twang marks someone as a hick who should be mocked. *Deliverance* does not exist in a vacuum.

My mother's family springs from this setting. The isolation and suspicion that inform the region also inform generations. It is coded in our genes like brown hair. For decades, outside help was never sought. Nor was it even imagined to be needed. My family tree kept growing inward, as each successive batch of children convinced their spouses, who were also from the region, to keep these matters within the family. Tighter and tighter the tree grew, and few people saw a need to thin the branches to let in a little nourishing light.

This cautionary tale is my attempt to do a little pruning. This is my attempt to untangle my family's history of mental illness. It is a story of mothers and daughters as well as a journey in search of absolution. It is about being at your most unbalanced when the rest of society expects you to be at your most joyful. It is about living in and with mountains, with occasional lapses into blue-grass and banjos. The past must be understood and, in some sense, loved, in order to be overcome.

Here is where my maternal great-grandmother abandoned her three children. Here is where my maternal grandmother went quietly mad. Here is where my uncle came home from Vietnam, put his gun to his head, and killed himself. And here is where my mother met my father, and then escaped the geography but not the heredity. Years later, I would be back in the same scenery, if a few miles farther south. The irony is not lost.

For six weeks after my birth, my mother didn't wash her hair. Now, she claims that she was postnatally splendid, except for that one little detail. Her assurances don't . . . assure. At the time of my birth, which was in the early 1970s, little was known about postpartum depression and even less could be done about it. My mother's interior landscape has always been a mystery to me and I didn't understand that her black moods weren't the norm. My childhood wasn't spent around happy families, against whom I could compare my sad home. Even in a big city, Mom and I remained more or less isolated. One of my fondest memories is of listening to my mother breathlessly sob on the other side of her bedroom door. There was nothing I could do, and, in so many ways, it was all my fault.

I swore I would not do the same to my daughter, yet, for two weeks after her birth, I did nothing but cry and, eventually, completely came apart like a wet tissue. My mother contends that this happened because I waited until my early thirties to have a baby and, in her words, "worked for too long" before fulfilling my biological destiny. My mom has never quite come to terms with the concept of women with careers. In her eyes, jobs are just what you have before you have a baby and your life becomes bliss. We all construct our own versions of reality in order to deal with the day, but this reinvention makes my eyeballs ache. If my birth caused bliss for my mom, please let me never find it for myself.

In many ways, my depression was the end state of an almost perversely natural progression. Not only is my family history shot through with crazy, but there had also been warning signs before I gave birth. My teen years had been full of undiagnosed fits of melancholy that went beyond what one would normally expect from a girl that age. In my early twenties, I scared the bejeezus out of a psychiatry intern by bursting into tears in her office and not being able to stop. There were signs, all right. The big red ones that signal danger.

1

Discovering the absolute beginning is like playing Pick Up Stix. Each object touches another. Isolating the events is impossible. And my hands have never been steady.

But I suspect that the beginning of the story of my family's madness lies somewhere in the landscape, like a picture of a ball of yarn hidden in a picture of Monet's *Water Lilies* in *Highlights* magazine. My mother's childhood landscape is harsher than my father's, even though it begins less than two hundred miles to the south of his.

Parkersburg, West Virginia, was built on oil, natural gas, and chemistry. Until the late 1800s, this wee settlement just over the river from Marietta, Ohio, was known more for farming than for industry. Now, the drive down Route 7, which flanks the Ohio River, passes enormous, rusty factories that squat on every vaguely flat piece of land. You can guess the plant's output by the smells. The polymer refinement company reeks of acetone and other volatiles. The coal-fired electric station is marked by sulfur. The only ones I can't pin down are the strange organic odors that waft from a nondescript factory that nuzzles up to a steep cliff. There is no sign to hint at what is being processed.

Every time I've driven this road, it has always been full of timber trucks and the sky, overcast with a threat of rain. My dad, who met my mom in Parkersburg while he was working for DuPont, recalls that he always knew when he was close to the city because the smog from one of these outlying plants obscured the road. One of my distant great-uncles also remembers that the stinks and haze were constant until they had made it through Charleston, beyond the Union Carbide plant that continually spewed fug into the air. West Virginia has long been a state that the rest of the country feels it is okay to abuse, either through a continual rape of the natural resources and residents or by constant scorn.

It rubs off, this feeling that the rest of the country doesn't give a damn about you. While the EPA has made minor inroads into cleaning the air, the image of the West Virginia hillbilly—that toothless, ignorant, incestuous, pipe-smoking dumbass—is impossible to shake. In fact, members of my mother's family still object to the title of this book. "We're 'mountaineers,'" they insist. "Not 'hillbillies.'" But because I am of a different generation, I am all about reclaiming words that have been wrongly sullied. *Hillbilly* is a perfectly fine word, one that captures the resourceful, gritty people who settled in the southern Appalachians and made unforgiving landscapes thrive while providing for the rest of the country. *Hillbilly* is nothing to be ashamed of—but until the words can be said out loud and with pride, the attitude will never change. For me, words like *bitch* and all of the descriptors for insanity, such as *crazy* and *lunatic*, fall into the same category. They are good words and I, for one, want them back on my own terms.

Reclaiming the word, however, is only the first step

and doesn't mean that the stereotype will fall. Witness this piece from March 2005's *Graffiti*, the alternative newspaper that serves Parkersburg, Charleston, and surroundings. On the front cover is West Virginia native Morgan Spurlock and inside is a screed by one Shelley McClain, a citizen railing about a recent bill that had been introduced into the state's legislature that will legalize public breastfeeding, a crime until then. McClain flames on abut how the bill's sponsors should have expected the public backlash because they are "fighting for the right to go against decency and self-respect and show the world their goods."

The fact that thirty-nine other states have such laws matters little to McClain, who feels that the state gets enough ridicule from the rest of the country. A woman feeding a child in the most natural way will merely confirm the state's Red State and redneck status. Also, McClain claims that tourists who see such things will insist that the state is still shackled by poverty. If parents have to rely on breast milk, clearly they are too poor to afford formula.

"Haven't we suffered long enough under the stereotypes and cruel jokes?" McClain asks. "We bring this crap on ourselves. No, it's not fair. It's not fair that other states like New York or Massachusetts or California could get away with something like this because they are stereotyped as higher class than us. But unfair doesn't make it OK."

If that's the way West Virginians perceive themselves now, imagine what it was like in the 1950s when my mother was a girl. Some things you never can quite shake and the stigma of growing up in a state stereotyped as backward is one of them. For example, when my parents married, Dad's coworkers gave him a glass desk blotter, which all of the men had signed with congratulatory notes and doodles. Someone—whose name is lost—drew a picture of my mother as the stereotypical hillbilly gal, buxom, barefoot, and in Daisy Dukes. It was thirty years before I realized that must have been insulting to her.

My grandfather, William Carl Tebay, was one of nine kids. The Tebay family is described in the Parkersburg papers of the time as "one of Wood County's oldest and most prominent families." My great-grandfather Amos is described in glowing terms, as is the dairy farm he started. The clan has been in the area near-on forever. Amos's father came to the region after the Civil War. Which side he was on or where he was before that is not remembered. My mother's wing of the family isn't the best at hanging on to that sort of information.

Most of Amos's boys went into business of some sort. The girls married well, including my aunt Donna, who was a free-spirited artist of the Georgia O'Keeffe school. Many of us in the family have at least one of her paintings, almost all of which feature flowers. Mine is from her watercolor period, a calla lily.

My mother is one of four children, three of whom (all of the girls, interestingly) are college graduates. The youngest sister—Linda—has an advanced degree. My mom is in the middle and Irene, who has always been called Snooks, is the oldest. The youngest sibling was my uncle Bill, who would have gone to college had he not been drafted to serve in Vietnam. He didn't live to see the end of the war, but didn't die directly because of it.

My grandfather William went to college and ran the Charleston branch of the Tebay family dairy for a few years, before packing up wife Nell, their son, and daughters to move to Grand Junction, Colorado, to prospect for uranium. No, really. Uranium. Apparently there was fine money to be made from radioactive elements in 1955. Ultimately, that didn't pan out, so the family returned to Parkersburg and moved into a nice house in a nice neighborhood, where they fit in fairly well. Yet things weren't quite right behind these closed suburban doors.

Until I had my baby, all I knew about my mother's mother was that her first name was Nell and that she had died of some female cancer when my mom was in college. My mother couldn't have an enameled metal turkey roaster in her house, because that is what my grandmother spent her last days vomiting in, which my mother would have to clean up. That was all that Nell meant to me: puke and cancer.

"I hated to come home," my mom told me once in a moment of rare candor, and she admitted that she had spent as much time at the university in Morgantown as possible. Nonetheless, she had had to leave school for a semester to care for Nell during her demise, one of my aunts informed me. My mother was the only one home when her own mother took her last breath. Nearly forty years later, my mother still won't discuss it.

Despite my mother's silence on the exact details, Nell's death in 1965 is more clear to me than her birth. For years, the family had celebrated her birthday as November 3, 1913. Years later, when Nell referred to the official copy of her birth certificate, the one the county had on file, she realized that it read September 12, 1912. The confusion isn't surprising. Her branch of the family—the Cains—is a mess to track. Nell's mother Elizabeth disappeared when her kids were very young and the three of them were raised by an aunt, whose true relationship to the family is unclear. Randomly, Elizabeth would return to Parkersburg for brief visits, then vanish again. Nell's father didn't stick around, either, and was last known to be working as a firefighter in Wheeling.

When news of Elizabeth's death reached her daughter, Nell and family were in Colorado. Nell herself hadn't been mentally well for quite some time. She was unable to keep her house marginally clean or her kids put together. The three girls learned quickly to take care of each other and their brother. Nell was better in the summer than winters, when she would stay stuck in the house during the dark days. Her presence was never intentionally toxic, and there were no harsh words or quick spankings, but it was a bleak atmosphere for her children. It wasn't encouraging or nurturing.

Her doctors had warned her not to have another baby after Linda, the youngest daughter, because with each pregnancy her moods grew less stable. Snooks can remember, as a kid, not being sure how long her mom would be in the hospital after each new baby. After Bill's birth in Charleston in 1947, depression smothered Nell like a wool suit on a hot summer day. For the next few years, she would be shuttled back and forth from Harding Hospital—a chichi loony bin in nearby Columbus, Ohio. A room at Harding wasn't cheap; nor were the shock treatments Nell received. Eventually, my grandfather ran out of cash to keep her there, after which, we think, my grandmother returned home to Parkersburg and Aunt Carrie acted as the family's housekeeper. Other friends and family provided support when they could.

After Nell returned to Parkersburg, she sank under the blackness, a chain-smoking zombie, made hollow by prescription drugs, electroshock, and depression. For a few years, she would follow her kids around the house, continually asking, "What are you gonna do now, honey?"

What they did was leave. Snooks married at twenty-one and had two babies. Soon Snooks's family would settle in South Carolina, where they lived in a gracious suburb with an enormous magnolia tree in their front yard. Snooks, for the record, strongly objects to my digging up nasty family laundry. As she told me at one point, "When you see shit, you flush it away." For me, this is only a reasonable response if you know your sewage system is up to the challenge. I'm fairly certain that ours isn't and I must deal with it in other ways.

At seventeen, Linda had gotten pregnant and married. She and husband, Steve, lived in Morgantown, where they struggled through college and parenthood. Always the sanest and most self-sufficient of the siblings, Linda has been sure and confident at all stages of her life. Even when her two grown daughters developed their mental illnesses, Linda was a superhero, swooping in to help. It is what she does.

On weekends, during Nell's final decline from cancer, my mother and Linda would switch places. Mom would escape to a boyfriend at WVU; Linda would come home to nurse. "It was such a hard time," my aunt recalls, welling up when she talks about it. The only child who was too young to get out was Bill. He would have remembered Nell's madness best, I imagine, but I never knew him. He blew his brains out a year before I was born.

All of this helps explain why it is so dang hard to piece together our maternal family history. Only since my daughter was born have I been able to make progress, mostly because my aunt's and mother's shock at seeing their own kids suffer from mental illnesses made them want to trace the source of that inclination, no matter how shameful it feels to expose. My father's side of the family is equally secretive about the twisted trunk of the ol' family tree, which is further complicated by immigration, language, and my paternal grandmother's freakish compulsion to throw away everything.

Slowly, though, it comes together. And as disturbing as the past can be, it is also reassuring in its explanation for how we got here.

I suspect the true beginning is lost in the seas of evolution. Somewhere, when the first apes were climbing out of trees, some mama ape went a little nutty after giving birth to a baby ape. The mama ape may or may not have survived, but the baby ape definitely did and the mutated bit of DNA was passed on to that baby ape's offspring. Over time, this maternal madness (as well as the systems that evolved to cope with it), became the norm for a great many families, no matter how many generations it took before all of them could walk erect. It's like the old Breck shampoo ads, where the one woman tells two friends, who tell two friends, and so on and so on. Except we're dealing with something a bit more serious than squeaky-clean hair here.

I am not an anthropologist. Nor am I a sociologist. I don't even play one on TV.

Journalist Andrew Solomon wrote an excellent study of almost every imaginable facet of depression called *The Noonday Demon* and is a much better researcher than I am. He writes:

> Is depression a derangement, like cancer, or can it be defensive, like nausea? Evolutionists argue that it occurs

much too often to be a simple dysfunction. It seems likely that the capacity for depression entails mechanisms that at some stage served a reproductive advantage. Four possibilities can be adduced from this. Each is at least partially true. The first is that depression served a purpose in evolution's prehuman times that it no longer serves. The second is that the stresses of modern life are incompatible with the brains we have evolved, and that depression is the consequence of our doing what we did not evolve to do. The third is that depression serves a useful function unto itself in human societies, that it's sometimes a good thing for people to be depressed. The last is that the genes and consequent biological structures that are implicated in depression are also implicated in other, more useful behaviors or feelings—that depression is a secondary result of a useful variant in brain physiology.

Of course, a discussion of the evolution of mental illness is only possible once you stop believing that madness is a curse sent by an angry God who wants to see you suffer simply because you made human choices. Or that it is a "choice" that you could resolve by taking vitamins and exercise, as a few "religious" leaders would claim through their actor mouthpieces. The evolutionary/biological components of depression have been recognized only in the last century, as medical advances have allowed us to look at the chemical/physiological origins of mental illnesses.

I can trace my family's evolution for only a couple of generations. On my father's side of my genetic code, we have a batch of Italians. My great-grandmother Mama Lane was from Naples and moved to Pittsburgh around the 1900s. She worked as a seamstress, when she wasn't

raising four kids, two of whom were from her first marriage (which left her widowed at a young age), two of
whom were from her second. Mama Lane, of course,
wasn't her given name, but a pet name bestowed upon
her by my dad, who, as a young child, couldn't pro-
nounce "Magdalena."

For almost a hundred years, Pittsburgh's mills were
attractive to immigrants. Without them, most of the
other industrial cities like Cleveland, Detroit, and Buffalo
wouldn't exist, either. During the boom times, when the
mills were pouring out millions of tons of steel, coke, and
iron, these cities were the center of the industrial universe. Now, they are part of the Rust Belt, struggling to
figure out what comes next. The manufacturing jobs
have moved on to other countries where the labor is
cheap and relatively naive. Pittsburgh can't keep its blue-
collar kids at home because there is nothing for them to
do anymore, unless they want to work in a Starbucks and
serve frothy drinks to college students and banking executives. The children of that immigrant base, whose lives
were dedicated to making tangible, useful goods, are slip-
ping away, moving to warmer climates and cities like Atlanta and Raleigh, where populations are growing fast,
although not because of manufacturing.

Still, the rumors of Pittsburgh's death are a bit pre-
mature. One of the country's hidden treasures, it gave the
world Andy Warhol, Mr. Rogers, and Billy Squier. The
views of the city alone are enough to make you swoon.
Most of the neighborhoods offer at least one high spot
from which to view the Point, which is where the Allegheny and Monongahela Rivers converge to form the
Ohio. The glass-and-stone skyscrapers rise majestically
from the enormous (and, it must be noted, phallic and

erupting) fountain on this pubiclike triangle of land. All pelvic references aside, one moment made me fall in love with the place. I was driving in from the airport after a few years of living in Tennessee. On one side of the mountains, it was gray and rainy, gloomy if typical weather. And then I drove into the tunnels and emerged on the other side, where the clouds had lifted. Bright sunshine was glinting off the steel buildings and metallic rivers. It was fall-to-your-knees gorgeous. It was Oz. Unfortunately, I still had to negotiate driving the bridges during rush hour, but the part of my brain that wasn't freaking out about traffic was enthralled.

Most folks who haven't been there conjure visions of a grimy, industrial center where thick-necked men drink cheap beer after their shifts. Pockets of this culture may still exist, but it is certainly a dated view. Thanks to many of the early industrialists who made Pittsburgh a steel powerhouse, most of whom came to believe in giving back to the folks whose sweat built their empires, Pittsburgh has a thriving intellectual community. Andrew Carnegie (the accent is on the middle syllable, contrary to what New Yorkers will claim) bequeathed the city a world-class library system, which has always been open to all residents, whether they labor in the mills, at a desk, or in a home. The Heinz and Frick families pumped millions into the cultural scene and their legacy continues to create benefits. Two major colleges—the University of Pittsburgh and Carnegie Mellon—are pioneering medical and robotic research. Pittsburgh encourages its residents to work hard and to be smart. It's hard to imagine that other cities currently being abused by wealthy industrialists will fare so well a hundred years from now.

But Pittsburgh, like most of Appalachia, is a place

that you really have to want to be in, despite its many charms. For me, there are always obstacles to a happy relationship with the city, no matter how much I may wax rhapsodic about it. For each positive, I have a negative. The winters can be brutal and gray. The city's topography—it evolved around three rivers and an imposing chunk of the Appalachians—makes it a pain to navigate through. Most denizens who learned to drive up the city's narrow streets and across its many bridges gave up on learning cardinal directions well before their seventeenth birthdays. You drive by feel here. By knowing which river should be on which side of your car, you know where you should be on any given hill. Once you stop wanting it to make sense, the way always becomes clear. Yet, even after twenty-some years of driving downtown from my grandmother's house, I always wind up in Dormont, an outlying suburb. This is equivalent to winding up in Seattle while trying to drive to L.A. from San Francisco. I have no explanation for this.

The geography of Pittsburgh has ensured that most of the neighborhoods stayed ethnically monolithic well into the late twentieth century; it was too bewildering to wander far from the set of streets that you knew well. Some would argue that these pocket communities still are remarkably homogenous for a city of its size. In my grandmother's day everyone in her neighborhood, Brushton, spoke Italian and came from the same region of the boot, more or less. If you crossed over the hill, you'd fall into an enclave of "hunkies," an ethnic slur for Hungarians, and "Bohemians," a label for those who emigrated from the Eastern European countries whose borders were constantly in flux, Poland, Czechoslovakia, and Albania. At that time, most of the people who came to the

Steel City were white, with waves of Romanians, Ukrainians, Scots, Germans, and the Irish making themselves at home. The African-American population was, for many years clustered in the Hill District, where nine of Pultizer prize–winning playwright August Wilson's dramas have been set. During the Jazz Age, greats like Billy Eckstine played on the Strip downtown.

In my great-grandmother's day, immigrants could live most of their lives without ever having to learn English or assimilate, especially if they had moved to the city when they were adults. By my grandmother's generation, this had changed, especially at the start of WWII. My grandmother tells me that businesses started hanging No ITALIANS signs shortly after the U.S. joined the fray. Even though kids from different ethnic neighborhoods went to the same schools and so were forced to mingle, there was still a stigma to being Italian. My grandmother's experience was typical of many immigrants. One language was spoken at home, another at school. Her friends all ate peanut butter while she ate macaroni and gravy. At a time of life when fitting in is the sole focus of a child's existence, she, like so many kids who are different, was an Other, trapped on the outside of the glass peering in.

One of the first things that Pittsburghers do when first meeting each other is ask what neighborhood they grew up in. Knowing that someone is from Bloomfield, say, or Sewickely, is a clue to what her history could be. It can tell another 'burgher who their grandparents might have been or whether they'll have pierogi for dinner. Just as a stranger holding forth on the finer points of grits identifies him as having lived in the South, a stranger who talks about jumbo or city chicken has steel city in his blood.

The Brushton neighborhood has morphed from an Italian enclave to a quasislum, yet the work of the Martini side of my clan is still evident. My father's father, along with his three brothers, were the core of Martini Brothers Construction, who also built the family house on South Wheeler Street. Each brother had his own specialty—carpentry, stonework, or plaster. My grandfather was a stone mason, and during World War II built runways for American planes on the island of Sabu. He died when my father was barely a teenager and, shortly after, my grandmother, father, and his younger brother moved out to Penn Hills, a western suburban.

Technically, I can't claim Pittsburgh as my hometown. Once he graduated from Pitt and worked for DuPont as a chemical engineer, Dad was transferred every couple years. I was born in Wilmington, Delaware, and then moved to Atlanta and Chicago, then back to Pittsburgh, all before I started first grade. After my parents divorced when I was eleven, Mom and I moved out to West View, a turn-of-the-century getaway for city dwellers that had then featured a trolley park and a roller coaster. A blue-collar enclave in an industrial city, West View in the eighties was waking up to the fact that it needed to redefine itself. Every third business was a pizza joint or a bar, and the bakery specialized in both *pizzelles*, an Italian wafer cookie, and *chrusciki*, a Polish fried dough cookie. By the time I lived there, the amusement park had been replaced by a Giant Eagle supermarket, a Kmart, and fast food. The city proper was a fifteen-minute bus ride away.

West View will always remind me of suicides. Self-destruction was in the air in those days. In my mind's macabre slideshow of memories, the first slide is of a walk home with a girlfriend. On the main drag, just in front of the dance studio where another friend taught, a car was parked, a late-model gas-guzzling something or other. Its windows were shattered and there was blood all over the driver's side. We stopped for a minute but a cop, stationed next to it, hurried us along, offering no details. On the evening news, we learned that the estranged husband of a nearby office worker had waited outside for her shift to end. When she left the building, he screamed obscenities at her to get her attention, then popped back into the car and shot himself.

Second slide is a junior high winter. A big, bumbling, greasy-haired kid who Mom and I knew, who was so massively insecure in his own skin that physical mayhem followed him everywhere, went out to shovel the walk. He took a handgun with him. When his dad got home from work, his only child was dead in the snow from a self-inflicted bullet to the head. White snow. Red blood. Dark skies.

The third and last slide is of R. Budd Dwyer, a Republican who had served terms in both the Pennsylvania House and Senate and was the state treasurer in 1987. Convicted of agreeing to accept kickbacks from a tax overpayment by state employees, Dwyer called a press conference the day before he was to be sentenced, presumably to resign. At the time this was such a huge case that all of the media was covering it live. Dwyer spoke for a bit, again protesting his innocence, then handed out three envelopes to three of his staffers; one contained a letter for his wife, another his organ donor card, and the third a letter for Gov. Bob Casey. Dwyer then opened a fourth envelope, pulled out a .357 Magnum, warned the assembled that the next bit might be upsetting, and blew his brains all over the curtain behind him. I would keep coming across R. Budd while in journalism school, since his messy death was always used as a talking point about media responsibility in the pre-9/11 world.

My own flirtations with death were minor. I'd stick pins into the tips of my fingers to see how far I could push them before I felt something. I spent a summer trying to starve myself, to see if anyone would notice. For three months I ate only 380 calories per day, which amounts to six saltines or a small bag of M&Ms, the number gleaned from a teen magazine that my best friend/next-door neighbor and I had bought to ogle pictures of Duran Duran. Despite the number of compliments I received on my new, skinny self, I eventually got hungry for real food again. My short attention span is a good thing, sometimes.

Yet on its surface, West View was no more depressing than anywhere else. The workers' kids went to North Hills High School. The township closest to it was Ross, which was exponentially more upscale than West View and also fed into the same school. You could usually pick which side of town each kid was from. Those with jean jackets and big hair were from West View. Those with Izod shirts and designer jeans were from Ross. You could almost hear the music from *West Side Story* as you walked through the halls. West View kids always knew they were destined for manual labor and sad, old houses stacked almost on top of each other on the city's hills. Ross kids could count on college and yards big enough to play soccer in.

Of course, there were those of us who, in high school, simply didn't give a rat's rump what was expected of us. I was one of those kids, rebelling against the high school cliques and status quo, the mousy, rumpled kid who sat in the corner letting her dry-as-toast comments fly among her few trusted friends. That's when I bothered to go to school at all. Given how depressed my mom was throughout most of my high school years—she was often out with a boyfriend, at work, or unconscious in her room—it was fairly easy to stay at home and watch MTV all day. Physically being in the school took too much energy. Most of my classes bored me and were easy to keep up with on my own time. As a "gifted and talented" kid, I was expected to constantly push myself for the sheer love of learning, but that took too much energy, too. I made no effort to challenge myself by taking harder classes.

Because of an admissions professional who must have been on narcotics, I was accepted to Allegheny College, a reasonably prestigious liberal arts college frequently touted as "Little Ivy League." Allegheny is hidden in the nondescript town of Meadville, Pennsylvania, which is itself hidden in the nondescript central section of the state. Because they offered the most comprehensive financial aid package, I matriculated there. While half of the students' parents were able to pay for four years in cash upfront and buy Muffy a new BMW to drive during her tenure, the other half of us came from modest means. Because of the number of grants and other help I had, my $80,000 education cost about $20,000, which I finished paying for a decade after graduating.

It was, however, worth every penny, even with the compound interest tacked on. When most of your classes contain fewer than twenty-five people, it's hard to go unnoticed. Professors pushed me until I felt like I was sure to break; then pushed me a little more. Four years there were exhausting and rigorous and giddy fun. While my degree is useless on a practical level—I have a BA in theater—it was invaluable on a developmental level. I eventually understood that learning stuff could be cool when the people teaching you really enjoyed their jobs and had no qualms about firmly kicking your ass when you gave up prematurely.

What helped the most, however, was just getting away from my mother. By the time I was finishing high school, it seemed to me that my mom had pretty much checked out of our relationship, investing herself instead in a series of odd boyfriends—one was a pool hustler; another, a butcher—whose attention kept her misery at bay. By this point, we were also on our fifth or sixth dog. Each would last about eighteen months before it disappointed her in some way, by either growing out of puppyhood or peeing on the rugs. The last dog was a Chihuahua who liked to bite us if we startled it. And, for the record, Chihuahuas startle easily. I still have scars. Our life together had no real constant, given the parade of boyfriends and dogs and moods. You just never knew what you'd get when you walked in the door, the silence of a completely empty apartment or soul-wrenching sobs or wounded anger over a perceived slight, like not putting my cereal bowl in the dishwasher because I hated her. College was a refreshing change. I could breathe, finally.

The transition, however, both sucked and blew. My mom hated Pittsburgh but stayed because she couldn't bear to take me away from my father, which always comes up whenever we talk about how miserable my high school years were. All of her bad moods and disappointments during her Pittsburgh years were my fault. We had to be there because I foolishly loved my father. Baptists can be martyrs, too.

All of my senior year, Mom went on about her plans to move to Central Florida, where her sister Linda and father now were. She didn't delay, either. The night before my commencement, she and my aunt packed up the apartment. After my congratulatory postgraduation lunch, at which my parents were able to remain civil, she hopped in her car and drove away. As she hugged me. I couldn't stop crying, even though by that point we were barely speaking to each other. My own mother couldn't wait to get away from me, proof that I was the least lovable child in the history of children. I didn't sleep at all that night, in my room at my dad's, where I would live for the next few months, until college started. I spent the summer working at one of three jobs, saving up cash for school. It was a colorless time, like when Dorothy goes from Kansas to Oz, but in reverse. I filled the void with massive amounts of fried food and ice cream, one sometimes dipped in the other.

When I was a kid, the mother/daughter relationship was easy. Mom was the center of my life and I listened to her. I would hide under her pink gingham housecoat when I was afraid. Her legs looked like they stretched forever in the diffuse light and cozy warmth. In college, at first, I would have weeks where I wanted to do nothing but be back under there, safe in the knowledge that my mommy would protect me from the world.

No one key incident marked the beginning of the end of our talking. Most of it was just preteen stuff, the kind of puberty-induced weirdness that plagues all families but which my mother took personally. But there were small betrayals, too. One of her boyfriends was a real peach of a guy who drove a fast car with an automatic transmission.

I didn't like him. My mother's theory, which she borrowed from Phil Donahue or another great sage, is that I wouldn't have liked anyone she dated because I felt a misguided loyalty to my unsupportive shit of a father. That's really not it, I'd explain over and over and over. Grocery guy was just slimy. But she sticks to her piece of pop psychology and I stick to my assessment. Since everything I say to him is interpreted as sarcastic or over his head (which was not inaccurate), I've learned to not speak when I'm forced to go somewhere with them. I get labeled as sullen.

One sweltering late-summer evening, my best friend/next-door neighbor and I decide to hop the fence at our apartment complex's swimming pool and take a clandestine dip in the pool to cool off. It was something other people frequently did and was tacitly approved of by the management. So we mention our plan to our folks—her parents and my mom and the aforementioned grocery guy—who give their approval and stand on our communal front porch to watch.

I try to climb the fence first. And don't make it over because, by this summer, I am well into my food-is-comfort phase and have moved from husky into full-blown fat. Coupled with this is my natural lack of athletic prowess. At best, I am graceless under pressure and trip over lines on the linoleum if I know anyone is watching me walk across the room. I knew they were all watching me fail. And I could hear them laughing.

So I waddle back to my mom, seeking a moment where I could metaphorically hide under her housecoat. "You're just a baby elephant," the boyfriend says. He's laughing so hard, he's crying. My mother says nothing.

Variations on the scene play out for the next decade

or so. It adds up. I don't talk because everything I say makes it worse. She never stands up for me. A thousand betrayals without apologies. Neither one of us is happy with what's here but neither one of us can let go. It's like we're locked onto each other's wrists, spinning in circles, faster and faster. If one lets go, we'll both fly off into oblivion. We can only define ourselves by this constant tension of being trapped and dizzy and without recourse. It's a hell of a way to grow up.

Many years later, a good friend of mine, Steph, and I were dishing about a third friend, Shelley. Steph and I both are products of indifferent mothering. Over coffee one morning, one of us brought up Shelley, about how she and her mom have a relationship that is truly loving and supportive. They hug and kiss and talk. They honestly enjoy each other's company. And Steph says, "It's like watching an exhibit at the zoo."

2

The closer I come to having my baby, the family curse, which my husband and I have joked about on many occasions, becomes less funny.

We'd always intended to breed but had not found the right time to do so during the eight years of our marriage. Two years previous, we had earnestly started talking about it, and so I'd weaned myself off of antidepressants. It seemed like a wise move before having a baby, and I was feeling more or less okay, psychologically. The dark moods and heart-clenching anxiety that had haunted my early twenties had been pushed out by minor career coups and a move to Tennessee. Besides, Scott and I had been together for more than a decade. We owned a house and good china. We flossed regularly. We were adults, finally, and not getting younger.

But the events of 9/11 pushed us over the edge. Scott and I are not unique in our reaction to that national horror. Something about the thought of life ending so stupidly, about the constant threat of opening an anthrax-laced letter inspires thoughts of procreation in the minds of the country's couples. When newsmen tire of reporting on the tragedy, they focus on the baby boomlet that is brewing. Color us trendsetters.

On Scott's October birthday, we decide to start trying, figuring that it'd take a year or so for me to actually conceive. Our hopes aren't high, given all of the infertility horror stories floating around on the network news and in women's magazines. We think this will take years and heroic measures and test tubes and white coats and profound despair and epic struggles, but we will put on a brave face. We can, at least, say we gave it our best.

Four weeks later I am about to enjoy my annual Pap smear. I'd skipped out of work early to go on a Wednesday afternoon, the one usually dead time at the scrappy weekly paper where I was writing and editing. All it took to get the time off was the mere mention of gynecology to the boss man. Had I brought up speculums, I could have gotten a raise. Sometimes, being one of the few women on the editorial staff has its advantages. So I take off before lunch with promises to be back before a 2 p.m. meeting.

"I think I might be pregnant," I tell the nurse, who stops pulling sample bottles of KY jelly out of a drawer. I'm sitting on the table in a paper gown, which tears every time I shift and exposes my bottom a little more.

"Did you take a home test?"

"No," I say.

"Isn't the suspense killing you?"

"No," I say. And it wasn't. My attention span has always been less than epic. I find it hard to finish a box of cereal before I get bored with it. Both the spouse and I are baffled by the fact that our relationship has lasted more than a decade, since I tend to wander off when any novelty fades. Four weeks into the baby-trying and the bloom was off the rose. Thoughts of a baby were inducing knee-locking terror, frankly, and I was pondering calling off this little biology experiment.

Signs had already begun, however. A few days earlier, at a friend's wedding, my first sip of wine had almost come back up and I surrender the glass to a coworker. My stomach roils all evening, soothed only with cake, pumpkin risotto, and fresh air. I'd been exhausted all week, yet couldn't sleep and would lie on the bed like a woman at sea, woozy and rocking on invisible waves. I start to down Pepto-Bismol, but it doesn't even touch the malaise.

"Do you want to be pregnant?" the nurse asks, timidly, as if a woman who doesn't want to breed shouldn't admit it in public, like I was farting at my grandmother's funeral. She sends me to the bathroom to pee in a cup. I put my clothes back on, first.

She comes back in, clutching a book and a stack of yellow paper. "Congratulations!" she beams.

"Now I have to go through with this," I start to say, then catch myself. I should say something memorable, like "one small step" or "I'll be back" or "thousand points of light." Something. But nothing comes. I sit there, in that antiseptic room on the table with the stirrups, and stare at the nurse, who is smiling like she'd just won the lottery. Eventually, she gets uncomfortable and leaves.

My doctor, a petite woman with a mass of curly brown hair, comes in. "Is this good news or bad news?" she asks.

"Good," I say, and it is. "I'm just surprised." I explain the whole thing, how we didn't expect it to happen so quickly and the World Trade Centers and the Pentagon and the threats of imminent attack and the second thoughts.

"Same thing happened to me," she says (for a brief instant I think she's pregnant, too), "when my grand-

father died. My daughter is eight now. Best thing that
could have happened." She outlines the dos and don'ts of
the next few weeks. Don't touch cat litter. Don't eat runny
cheese or cold cuts or take hot baths. Stop the round-the-
clock Pepto. Do eat a balanced diet and take prenatal vitamins. Baby is due at the beginning of June. All of this is
on the yellow sheets of paper, which I dutifully gather up,
along with a book that has a soft-focus cover image of a
naked and radiant new mom and her naked and radiant
babe. There are a couple of free magazines, which also
feature radiant new moms, but no nudity. And so begins
my initiation into the cult of motherhood. *Radiant* appears to be the password.

I don't really remember the drive from the hospital,
where my OB's office is, back downtown to work. My
first stop was my office, where I called my husband.

"So?" he says.

"Yeah," I say.

"Wow," he says.

And then we don't say anything for a bit.

"How do you feel?" he says.

"I don't know," I say. And I don't. I should be jumping
up and down and kissing strangers. Instead, I'm staring
out the window, phone to my ear, and watching the pigeons on the ledge. I ponder going out to sit with them,
my legs dangling into the October chill. Instead, I go to a
meeting, where I avoid everyone's eyes while we talk
about editorial budgets and local gossip. I know I'm sitting on a nugget of info that will eventually make the gossip rounds, if only in a small way. My life has never been
interesting enough for the local rumor hounds to sniff at
my heels. I am boring on so many different levels.

*   *   *

I start reading everything I can get my hands on, from *What to Expect When You're Expecting*, which makes me feel guilty because I'm not existing solely on a diet of unprocessed brown rice and free-range carrots, to *The Girlfriend's Guide to Pregnancy*, which leaves me laughing so hysterically that I can't always stop. I also can't read past the chapters on the first fourteen weeks. If anything, my reading has convinced me that most pregnancies are doomed. Mine feels doubly so since it happened so easily. This baby should have been something I had to earn.

By Thanksgiving, my all-time favorite holiday because it is based around my all-time favorite foods, my stomach will tolerate only five items: mixed nuts (which have to be Planters' vanilla roasted), cranberry juice, canned tuna, butter, and bread. Everything else either violently comes back up or makes me so queasy that I wish it would violently come back up. The prenatal vitamins are the worst. I've taken to choking them down before bed, opening the cap while holding my breath because the mere smell triggers gagging. All night, the vitamins lie in my belly like rocks.

Shortly after turkey day, a big-name magazine editor calls to give me some good news. An interview that I had pitched on Alton Brown, food show genius, is a go. If I play it right, this wee little interview might be a springboard to future (and lucrative) freelance projects for this publication and its sisters. I'd never really intended to become the sort of writer who could churn out sassy bites of information for obscene amounts of money. I fell into the business, in fact, because I didn't get into grad school (twice) and dropped out of massage therapy school (once). While the act of writing itself has never been easy, it is quite possibly the only thing that I've ever done that feels like the right thing to be doing while I am doing it. I have never felt guilty for taking the time to write—notable because I feel guilty for almost everything else I spend my time on, from reading to cleaning to eating. Plus, every now and again, perhaps when Jupiter aligns with Uranus, the act of writing is also rewarding on some mystical level.

Every now and again it is also rewarding on a financial level. The Alton Brown piece would certainly buy a lot of diapers. There's only one problem: in order to do the interview, I'm going to have to drive down to Atlanta. It's only four hours from Knoxville, but it seems like an insurmountable obstacle when I can barely keep down cranberry juice. By the morning of the interview, I'm a mess and sit on the edge of the bed shaking, a symptom of queasiness and dizziness, from the shame of no longer being a competent adult who can drive a car for four hours.

The Hub takes pity on me, calls in sick, and drives the car. I spend the trip freaking out about meeting a TV ministar and then about how I will keep from throwing up on his shoes. Once we make it to a fabulous restaurant in the nouveau riche section of Atlanta, I escape to the bathroom to gather my scattered wits. It's a tasteful little room, all done in black Labradors and plaid. I can't imagine the ladies who use the facilities even tinkling on these pristine commodes, much less leaning their heads on the cool porcelain and dry heaving. I can no longer even pretend that I know what I'm doing.

The interview, however, goes smashingly well, mostly because Brown is a damn nice guy who has a knack for setting twitchy reporters at ease. There is a small contretemps when I refuse his generous offers of bites of his food. I'd picked the blandest items on the menu and could just barely look at his exotic seafood club without heaving. I want to explain the whole thing, that I'm not really like this, that this sweaty, jumpy woman isn't really me, that I'm pregnant and queasy and overwhelmed. Brown would understand. He'd give me a hug, pat me on the back, let me rest my head in the nook of his shoulder, and tell me it would all be okay. And I'd believe him, because he is a TV food guy and, therefore, trustworthy and infallible, much like the late Pope or the equally late Peter Jennings. I say nothing, instead, and secretly wonder if I am going to be this needy for the duration of the gestation.

Only one person besides Scott knows about my delicate condition. A woman I work with—let's call her Diane— catches me as I'm coming out of a stall in the office loo. "Can I tell you something? A secret?" she says. "I'm pregnant, due in early July."

"Congratulations!" I say, and mean it. It had been a rocky baby-making road for her and her husband, both of whom desperately want to be parents. They strike me as more fit for babies, mostly because they are Republicans, than Scott and I.

"But don't tell anyone," she says. "We're not telling anyone yet."

"I won't," I say, "and let me tell you a secret. I'm pregnant, too."

"Congratulations!" she says, and, I assume, means it. I don't tell her how quickly it happened and how I'm still a bit stunned and unworthy and woozy. Diane positively glows, now that I look at her. I look like phlegm.

Since I am convinced that I'll miscarry during my

first trimester, we don't tell our parents until just before Christmas. I have decided to take to my bed for the day because I'm too woozy to be of any use. Our bedroom is decorated in a style I call Early Tenement. Smoodges of dried panel adhesive dot the walls, which also have big gouges in the plaster where we've tried to remove these stubborn glops left over from a hideous 1970s renovation that involved faux-pine paneling covered by textured wallpaper. For the last four years we've been working on our charming fixer-upper, trying to undo all of the damage that the previous owner had wrought. We have managed to complete only the bathroom and figure the "nursery" is the new priority. But our personal sanctuary will have to wait—and I heave a little suffering sigh each time I clap eyes on the walls of the "master" bedroom.

We call my mother, who is beside herself with glee. She then starts to tell me about my birth, about how my father was a real shit during labor. When she winds down and rings off, Scott calls his folks—we're certain we can hear his mother's whoops of joy from Upstate New York even without the aid of the phone. I'm fine, I'm fine, I assure everyone when they ask how the first trimester has gone. I'm just a little woozy.

I call my father. I don't want to tell him, strangely, as if letting him know I'm pregnant is tantamount to having sex in front of him. It's not that my father is a prude, just that I've always been nervous to be a grown-up around him. When Scott and I moved in together, my father went ballistic. "It's not what good girls do," he said. I lacked the balls at that point to remind him that it was no longer 1953. Regardless, I don't even like kissing Scott in front of my dad. Telling him I'm knocked up makes me feel fourteen instead of thirty, like I'll be grounded. My father is, of course, thrilled, although he doesn't emit eardrum-smashing whoops of joy. My relief is accompanied by a wave of vertigo, and I flop back down on the bed and wait for it to pass.

The next day, I tell my boss, who is also elated.

"So you are coming back after the birth?" he asks, after an appropriate amount of pregnancy-related questions.

"Of course," I say. The idea of staying home with the tot lacks appeal, but I don't tell anyone this. For my generation, who were weaned on Susan Faludi and *Bust* magazine, it's hard to know how one should do the mom thing. There is only one rule anymore, which is that you will be shunned in any given circle no matter what you choose to do. Some of my friends would be appalled that I don't want to breast-feed for five years and homeschool. Others would be pissed that I didn't immediately go from delivery room to conference room. And yet there's still more shame than ever attached to admitting that I would rather be dipped in hot lava than be a full-time mom. Like I shouldn't even be having kids in the first place.

"Good," my boss says. And we're done.

News travels fast in Knoxville. Most folks with a bohemian bent know one another. By the turn of the year, my secret isn't one. I don't care, really, but am getting tired of always acting elated every time someone congratulates me. I want to tell them the truth, that I'm sick and scared, that I didn't quite realize how damn physical this whole baby thing would be. In the last dozen weeks, I've lost eight pounds. I don't really sleep deeply anymore and only doze for an hour or two at a time, then stare at the ceiling until it's time to go to work. No one wants to hear this. They want joy, which I give them, or I just say that I'm fine and move on.

*   *   *

The exam room is dim during my first sonogram, with the only light pooling around a computer station, where there is one monitor. I lie on what looks like a dentist's chair and push my pants down enough to expose my belly. The tech squirts lukewarm Ghostbusters' slime all over it and starts running a cigarette pack–sized receiver through the goo. The Hub and I can see all of this on the second monitor, the one that is above my feet.

And then we see a blob of phosphorescing dots on a screen. Here is a little hand, with five fingers, waving. Here is a tiny foot. There is a weeny skull and a blur of a face. We have made this little person. It is profound. Most telling is that I can't even come up with a clever little analogy for how gobsmacked we are. We simply watch with our mouths hanging open, letting in flies. I don't love the baby then, but I am amazed by biology.

The tech is capturing screen shots and computing measurements. All seems to be in order. Then she says, "Do you want to know the sex?" We do, going on the theory that the fewer surprises there are in the delivery room, the better. "It's a girl," she says, and shows us the baby has her legs up and open, giving us the perfect shot of her crotch. "I hope she isn't doing that as a teenager," Scott says, nervously. And we all laugh.

The lights are flipped on and I'm given a wad of paper towels to mop up the goo. (The wad is inadequate and I spend the rest of the day pining for clean underpants.) Pictures of the sonogram images are handed to us, as is the video, which is now full of what we were seeing during the last fifteen minutes. We leave the office with our arms around each other and float back to our jobs.

"Look, look!" I grab the first person I see and flap the pictures in front of him. "There's a little hand. There's a little skull. How cool is this?"

My boss is looking at me like I've spent my morning smoking crack. "It's great," he says. "How can you tell that's a skull? It looks like a hamster."

The women in the office see it immediately and are dutifully excited, circling me like a litter of puppies, eager to sniff my most recent treasure. I give up on the guys. Poor things. The Y chromosome sucks out their sense of romance.

"Don't you just love her?" Diane asks me a week and a half later, after she has had her first sonogram. She's having a girl, too. Everyone in the office now knows about her blessed event as well. On the whole, we are polar opposites in terms of handling the whole gestation thing. She panics at the slightest twinge and rushes to call her doctor. I feel guilty because I tend to ignore just about everything but outright pain and fear that this will make me an uncaring mother, just like my mother and her mother before her.

"Of course I love her," I say. But that's not true. I haven't felt some upswelling of maternalness, where I gaze serenely at every small child and rush to wipe her nose. What is true is that this whole baby thing is now real to me. There is a person in there and, eventually, she's going to want out.

By February, even my fat clothes won't fit. One advantage to my having explored a wide range of weights over the last decade is that I always have something to wear, no matter what shape I currently hold. None of my normal clothes, however, are designed for a body that is rapidly becoming one of Dr. Seuss's Sneetches. By this point, even the size 16s won't meet around my middle and the big shirts button only to the bottom of my rib cage. And, so, into the maw of hell that is the modern maternity shop.

Yes, I know that togs for the pregnant set have greatly improved in the last thirty years. And, yes, I know that my generation is lucky, that mothers past had to make do with belly bows and Empire waists, which they had to walk for miles through deep snow to purchase, uphill both ways and barefoot. Yes, I thank my stars (or, at least, I would if I knew how) that I am pregnant now, in a time when double-knit polyester is shunned for the aberration that it is.

Still, the clothing options are not vast for the knocked-up, especially the knocked-up who aren't willing to fork over obscene amounts of cash for something to wear for just a few months. At the mall, my shopping options are limited to one store, which is so packed with froufrou monstrosities that it is like shopping in Stevie Nicks's closet. I am the only one there alone. Two giddy young women—they can't be more than twenty—are with their mothers, who keep flinging more outfits over the changing stalls' doors. "Here, honey," they implore, "this'll look so cute." And, without fail, these tiny-tummied girls look adorable, like poster children for the maternal glow. They are radiant.

I sit in my stall—the big handicap-accessible one, which is the only changing room not occupied by these mother-daughter pairs—and try on the same outfits, hoping a bit of adorable comes my way. But adorable is harder to find once you're over thirty. Nor is the cause helped by a rack full of outfits skewed toward the tweenie set. Others capture some sanitized ideal of what maternity should look like—bland, chaste, and functional, in a tasteful floral with a tummy panel. I look like a milkmaid, all frump and *Glamour* Don'ts.

What doesn't look ridiculous on me is simply enormous. I could smuggle watermelons in the overalls and can't ever imagine that they'll fit. Padded, detachable tummies hang in the changing room to be stuffed down the fronts of your outfits so that you can get a sense of what you'll look like in four months. They don't help at all. I can't ever imagine being large enough to fill out the circus tent I'm currently wearing.

I wish my mom were with me. This same strange melancholy, a vague feeling that my mother should be involved, descended on me while I was shopping for a wedding dress. It is a complete, hallucination-level fantasy, given that my mom and I have always disagreed on clothes and what makes me adorable. It's not actually *my* mother I want, not really. If she were here, I'd be sulking in the changing room while she sighed outside, practiced her martyr face, and complained about how difficult I am. While I know that my mom loves me, I strongly suspect that she doesn't like me very much. Really, I want Erma Bombeck or June Cleaver to come help me. You know, a "mom" who could scan the racks and find the clothes that would make me look adorable.

Before my actual mother found out she was going to be a grandmother, we'd reached a nice relationship plateau, which we'd managed by not talking to each other very much. This accord took most of my lifetime to achieve. At several points, I feared that I'd have to call in Jimmy Carter, who could broker a detente and bring us peanuts, all in the same visit. Instead, we got around the many, many emotional relationship swamps by shutting up. Dysfunctional yet functioning, for the most part.

But with the news of the impending grandbaby has come increased conversation. She has started to call weekly, asking about my nausea, then launching into one of many stories about how unpleasant my father was when she was pregnant. For each new milestone I have achieved, she has had to top it with a yarn about my insensitive pop. Her morning sickness tale revolved around a party they were supposed to attend. She felt too ill to go yet he forced her to anyway. And there she stood, green and exhausted, while he had a good time. If the Catholic Church knew of my mom, they would give her a feast day.

I vow, right there in the changing room, under the fluorescent lights, in my too-big overalls, that I will do this maternal dance perfectly. My girl-child and I will never drift apart. I will be with her when she buys her wedding dress and maternity clothes. She won't hate me. There will be no distance. I will be everything she could want for a mother, everything that I never had.

Like cellulite, dreams come easily.

During my annual pilgrimage to Atlanta's largest antiques show, I find the perfect prints for the baby girl's nursery. Whimsical fairies perch on flowers, delicate and sweet. I am sure the baby will be sweet and delicate as well. That is what babies are, after all.

I appraise every mother I pass. Some look like the ones on the magazines with angels strapped in strollers, bundles of joy who are content to watch the world go by. Some push writhing, whining anacondas, red-faced and undulating over the carriage's sides. My baby and I will be the former, of course. Perfect moms never get frazzled.

Scott and I dream about the nursery, which will take over my makeshift office space in the second bedroom, and concoct an infant fantasia of fairies and purples and twee. The realization of the fantasy requires hard work. My mother and stepfather drive up from Florida and help us sand walls, since the Early Tenement look is in full force in this room as well. Magically, Mom and I don't kill each other, but I think this is due more to everyone being completely worn out by sanding and painting and cleaning than by any great leaps in maturity.

Not even my mother's continual recitation of her Pregnancy Trinity gets on my nerves, further proof that those late-pregnancy hormones rival heroin when it comes to smoothing out life's rough edges. Her Pregnancy Trinity goes thusly: 1. My father wasn't very helpful. 2. She didn't wash her hair for a month or so after coming home from the hospital but was otherwise in the pink, mentally. And, 3. She was visited by an angel the night I was born.

To take the liturgy point by point:

1. No, my father wasn't very helpful. He and the OB spent the latter part of my birth describing the mechanics of a "force fit," the engineering definition of an object that can only pass through another object in a specific, difficult-to-achieve way. I can see how this conversation would be irritating to a woman in labor. But it was also 1971 and men in the labor room was a relatively new occurrence. I don't know that any of those guys had an inkling what they were in for, which doesn't excuse his general unsupportiveness, granted. My father didn't speak to my mom for a few days after my birth, just sat quietly in the corner, pale and mute. She has never for-

given him for that. It galls her that I don't hate him for that, too.

2. Her denials that everything was fine, except for the hair-washing thing, are hollow, somehow. I just don't believe her, since she has occasionally let slide tidbits of information like about how she had a brief moment when she thought about killing me. You know, little things like that are telling. But her story is that she was fine except for her hair. She's sticking to it. And I have already been too crappy a daughter to want to pry further into this.

3. By nightfall of the day I had been born, my mother was alone, curled up on her hospital bed and feeling the exertions of the day. She wants her mom, Nell, who has been dead for a few years by that point. A nurse comes in and starts rubbing her back and stroking my mom's hair, just like Nell used to. This nurse was my mother's angel, sent by her God to comfort her in this time of need. She devoutly believes this—that God goes out of his way to constantly soothe her path through life and, every now and again, speaks to her. Yet she constantly insists that *I'm* the one who needs therapy.

Perhaps the smartest thing the Hub and I do during this time is hire a doula. While *doula* sounds like something you'd order in a Greek restaurant—"I'd like a side of doula with my souvlaki"—a doula is a woman who comes with you to the labor room. Her sole task is to make sure the laboring mother gets all of the mothering she needs during the birth process. Our doula already had five children of her own (four of them without drugs, no less), which, together with her years of training, put her on top of the whole birthing business. I was relieved to know that she'd be there. Someone in the room should know what she's doing.

The doula was also a lactation consultant who would help me get the breastfeeding cha-cha-cha started. All of my college-educated bohemian buddies—very few of whom, I must observe, actually had kids at that point— told me that breast is best and chicks who formula feed are wimps who don't care enough about their infants' health to put up with a little discomfort. One possible wrinkle in my plan might be the breast reduction I'd had a decade before. But my plastic surgeon assured me that her technique usually allowed for future breastfeeding. The doula was fairly confident that we'd "get milk out" of me. So I bought nursing bras and a Boppy, a crescent-shaped pillow, in preparation.

I am running out of preparatory things to do when two of my girlfriends throw a baby shower. Suddenly, I am the center of attention, cooing over tiny clothes while the baby somersaults in my stomach. By now, I fit into maternity clothes with ease, my belly jutting out enough that I can rest a coffee cup on the shelf it makes under my breasts. I start to wonder if everything will ever fall back into its previous location.

My head feels like it is floating near the ceiling for most of the shower, tethered to reality only by my giant belly. It is like an out-of-body experience, but without the death and the white tunnel, or the sense of peace and the reunion of lost friends. I watch the tops of heads of my friends as I unwrap everything. "Aren't you thrilled?" they ask. "Of course," I say, lying though my teeth. "It's like a dream come true."

No one has asked who painted my dreams, however. And I don't volunteer the information because I don't want to muddy anyone's visions of what pregnancy should be. My dreams are more steel gray H.R. Giger than pastel Hallmark card. When I can sleep, all is blood soaked and violently erotic. But most nights, sleep is hard to come by. When I find a position that doesn't make my hips ache and start to drift off, the baby squirms and I'm again wide-eyed. I don't wake up Scott, who is working through his own fears and doesn't need me to add to them. I don't tell anyone. I am so ashamed of not being blissfully happy, of the darkness that is starting to lap up around me. Black circles under my eyes start to look like bruises. I am isolated by this big belly, which pushes the rest of the world away like waves breaking before the bow of the *Titanic*.

Distractions like the baby shower are welcome, even if I can't get excited about them. There isn't much else for me to do, really, other than brood. I can't read past the second trimester in the stacks of birth books I've amassed. I can't watch the middle bits of the labor-and-delivery shows on television, which is where they always stick the pain and the pushing and the gore. I home in instead on how happy everyone looks before and after the fact. Even when the birth is mere weeks away, I don't think about it, daydreaming instead about how great a mom I'm going to be and how happy I'll be once the baby is out of my body. My nights tell a different story, but I ignore them. Sleep deprivation makes it hard to concentrate on anything. I drift off in meetings, lost in reveries of how much more meaningful my life will be in a few short weeks. That's what all the glossy guidebooks tell me, that I will be fulfilled by a seven-pound bundle of pure joy on levels that I had never before dreamed. The exact mechanisms of how this will happen are vague. But the books can't lie, can't they?

My baby's birth made me less of a woman.

My doula and I made blue-sky plans. I would go into labor, shun all drugs because I am tough, and my child would be born after a few pushes and no episiotomy. Then like the Madonna, I would curl around my new joy, who would latch onto my breast, which would flow with milk like a creek after a summer storm. Women have been doing this for millennia. Surely I could do it just this once.

By the fifth laborless day after my due date, my sense of humor is as hard to find as shoes that fit my swollen feet. My toes look like Vienna sausages. The waiting makes me jumpy. Any minute now the ball could roll out. Every Braxton Hicks contraction makes me want to grab my bags and run to the hospital. But these little cramps never add up to anything but held breath and dashed hopes. Every other day I waddle in to see my OB, only to be told that nothing has changed.

"Everything hurts," I whine to the nurse practitioner. She simply shrugs at me, her body language clearly telling me to suck it up, loser. I almost launch myself at her throat, but I know she can outrun me. I remember a pregnant dog that lived at a B&B in Asheville, where Scott and I had escaped when I was eight months along to enjoy some alone time. The smallish dog looked like a weird beagle/dachshund cross. The poor thing was a week overdue, so bloated with puppies that her little feet could just barely reach the ground. She spent most of her time in our room, lolling on the floor and staring up at us with big watery eyes. "Just kill me," she seemed to be saying in her own doggie way. "Please kill me now. Or, if you won't kill me, please go get me some peanut butter crackers. Either is good."

My one solace is food. Anything that is good for me—like broccoli or bran flakes or tofu—makes me woozy. I start sucking down Oreos and cake frosting from plastic tubs. Some researchers suggest that a sugar addiction can be a sign of depression. For me, it simply was a way to distract from my constant anxiety. The cycle of sugar high then crash gives me something entertaining to do. I daydream about drinking beer and lying on my belly. Once the baby is out, I can sleep without a foot kicking my spleen. I fantasize about undisturbed rest like a teenager dreaming of rock stars.

I complain to my doula, who suggests I try black cohosh tea and evening primrose oil in order to induce labor, which I do, but they give me diarrhea. Everyone tells me that sex helps get the process rolling, but in my current state I feel about as sexy as the flu. Just pondering the topology of my body and the mechanics of sex wears me out, much to my husband's chagrin. Stranger home remedies are proposed: enemas, Mexican food, long walks. The drawbacks of each are legion.

I have nothing to do. I'm on maternity leave and have tied up every loose end so thoroughly that no one calls to ask questions, which is vaguely disappointing, like I'm not actually needed at the job I'd built my life around.

The baby clothes have already been bought, washed, and folded. Furniture has been assembled and the mobile hung. I try to read, but can't concentrate because I try to interpret every twinge as a sign. We are as ready as we'll ever be and, yet, nothing. Friends call to ask if I've had the baby. I don't rip the phone out of the wall because I wouldn't be able to get down on the floor to plug in a new one.

An induction is scheduled. My mother arrives about a week before the appointed date, on the off chance that something will happen before then. She and my step-father pull up their trailer from Florida and are living at a campground out in the East Tennessee countryside. Every morning my mother arrives at my house. She makes me lie down whenever I try to do something more taxing than sitting. I don't have the energy to fight her considerable will and retreat to the bedroom. The halcyon days of her previous visit, where we didn't yell at each other once, have vanished. Her every word is an ice pick to the temple. Whenever she launches into her account of the Trinity—my dad, her hair, and the angel—I want to pull a van Gogh and slice off an ear, so that she can carry it around with her and talk to it.

When my mother is not physically at our home, she calls with alarming frequency to make sure we haven't been sneaky and had the baby without her. On the day that I'm induced, she beats us to the hospital. Her excited hands are like butterflies, flapping all over the place, grabbing my things. I'm too terrified to be irritated anymore. I feel like a Pacific pearl diver, hyperventilating before a deep plunge.

We check in at midnight, gritty eyed from lack of sleep. I take off my clothes and tie on a hospital gown.

Scott and I take down the crucifix that is hung in our room (and every room, since this is a Catholic hospital). We put the anguished Jesus into the top drawer of the dresser, right next to the TV. Microphones are strapped to my belly and an IV is started. The nurse accidentally nicks another vessel while tapping the main one and blood starts running down my hand and onto the floor. I apologize for making a mess.

By twelve thirty, I'm feeling tiny contractions, as if a muscle is being flexed. It doesn't hurt at all. I start to think that this all might not be as painful as they say. The nurse turns off the light and orders us to get some shut-eye. The Hub is out in an instant. I lie in the dark and watch the monitor, one rhythmic line for the baby's heartbeat, one line for my contractions. We've got rhythm, the babe and I, and may crack the Top 40 one day. I stay like that until dawn.

By morning, the contractions have started to hurt a bit, like intense menstrual cramps. Scott is holding my hands and we are watching Wimbledon, which amuses my nurse to no end. My doula has moved me to a rocking chair and placed a warm compress on my lower back. With every pain I rock forward and back, forward and back. At times, I can match the pace of my rocking to that of a tennis rally, each solid thock of the ball coinciding with the sound of my feet hitting the ground. I don't know why it helps, but it does.

My mother comes in and tries to rub my back, but the doula, bless her, shoos my mother away, just like we'd asked her to. When the doula leaves my room to keep my mother informed of the progress, they pray together. I don't know what to make of this.

An hour or so after daylight, my OB comes by. She checks my cervix, which is the most painful part of the process so far, and suggests that she break my water and that I have an enema. And so she does, with a tool that looks like a crochet hook. After the initial gush, which feels like sitting on a warm water balloon, amniotic fluid continues to trickle out of me, running down my legs and into my socks when I get up to go to the bathroom. By this point, it is dawning on me that labor isn't as glamorous as it looks in movies.

Ten minutes later, the pain begins. Real pain, centered at the base of my belly, just above my pubic bone, it radiates out to my toenails and hair. Then it stops just long enough to offer a sweet taste of pain-free life, then starts again, more powerful than before. This must be what death feels like.

I try to breathe, to center on some distant damn happy place, but can't remember where I've put it. The insides of my legs are covered in all kinds of ick, squeezed out of me with each contraction. The doula is whispering in my ear, some hippie affirmation about experiencing only the moment I'm in and not focusing on the past or future and I'm trying to do this but I really just want to scream and hit and push and give this to someone else but I can't because it is mine, all mine, and it's what I deserve for not being nice to my mother and not being perfect and for making a mess and for not living up to expectations and for just being female. This will probably kill me, I think, and hope that it does so quickly. And I have a brief thought about the interconnection between death and birth. Then the pain starts again and all thought leaves, replaced by fear.

I am a failure. Rather than conquering the pain like a

real woman, I whimper for an anesthesiologist. While I have long joked to my friends that I wasn't set on a natural labor—after all, I don't do natural dentistry—begging for drugs feels like such a cop-out and bourgeois admission that I'm not as strong as I'd thought. I hate myself, right then, disgusted with my own frailty. I imagine that the doula and the nurse see me as weak and annoying.

The six or so contractions between my white flag and the cavalry's arrival are worse than the ones previous, now that I know I'm about to be rescued by a thin needle jammed into the space between two of my lower vertebra, an epidural. It's a crude but effective anodyne. While modern science has refined and redeveloped most other medical procedures, childbirth "comfort measures" (as health professionals euphemistically call them) haven't changed all that much. You either go natural or put a needle in your spine. We've come a long way, baby.

All of my friends had told me that, compared to contractions, an epidural isn't that bad. What they left out is that, compared to labor, being set on fire wouldn't be so bad. Having someone poke metal into your back still hurts, but at that point, if you thought it would make the pain end, you'd let someone stick a needle in your eye.

The anesthesiologist curls me up on the bed and snaps at me when I unfurl a bit during a contraction. I hold Scott's hands like he's the only thing keeping me tethered to the planet. The needle goes in, and it burns, and the drugs start. The relief is immeasurable. I start shaking and sweating and crying. Everyone pats my hands and tells me how brave I was and how strong. But I know they're lying. I'm a coward.

I don't tell anyone this and smile and nod and accept ice chips. For the next couple of hours, we watch tennis—although I'm finding it hard to follow the points. Every now and again the nurse comes in to increase the Pitocin and check my cervix. There is steady, if slow, progress.

By noon, Scott is starving. He's had one granola bar since six the previous night and is about to swoon from hunger. When the nurse comes back, he asks for an ETA, so that he can sneak out to grab a quick bite. She pokes at my cervix, which, strangely, still hurts, and asks him if he can wait about an hour, because the baby should be here by then.

And so I push. And push. And push. With each contraction, which I can feel again in a distant way, I push for a ten count. Then relax. An hour passes. Then two. My doctor comes in and mentions that the baby's head really hasn't moved at all, but that she's sure that I can push the baby out. Her confidence is oddly placed. What about me creates the impression that I am a champion pusher? She leaves. I feel like a slacker, like I'm too out of shape and lazy to get the job done. My mother pops her head in and asks what's taking so long. The doula steps out to explain and I'm certain she's telling her what a loser I am, how I've been kidding myself all along that I deserve to be a mother.

I am rolled onto my side and push from there. I am helped onto all fours and push from there. I am huge and clumsy and my legs don't want to hold my weight. A tray full of the instruments that will be needed once the baby crowns is brought in, then sits unused. Three hours pass. The phone rings. It is a woman from my office who tells me that Diane had her baby an hour ago, even though she was due two weeks after me. I hate her. Her early birth feels like a betrayal.

At the start of hour four, I can no longer open my eyes. When I feel a contraction, I sit up just enough to push, then fall back and semisleep until I have to push again. I will be doing this for the rest of my life, this pushing. I am helpless, a collector's butterfly, straining against the pins. Nothing ever moves. The baby's head is jammed in my pelvis but her heart is beating strongly and they are going to let me push forever.

"I can't do this anymore," I whisper. And with that sentence, the nurse calls my doctor, who rushes down, gloves up, and feels around in my vagina trying to figure out what is wrong. The baby, she discovers, is facing my left hip instead of facing my spine. Forceps are brought out and they do look like salad tongs, just like in the movies. One side of the tongs fits easily. The second doesn't. She keeps trying but is having a hard time getting them to close in a way that won't damage the baby's face. All of this rooting around in my pelvis hurts, like a dentist with enormous hands trying to rotate your back teeth with only his thumbs.

Eventually, she figures it out. The forceps are hooked together and I have to push again. And I do. My tiny doctor pulls. And I push again. She pulls again. And the baby's head moves, finally, then she gets stuck at the chest. The doctor mentions that she has never had that happen before. How nice it is to be a medical marvel. I push again. She pulls some more. The tight fit is unexpected. I'm not a small woman. My hips could kindly be described as child-bearing. Descriptions are horseshit.

I am given an episiotomy and my baby is pulled into the world. Opening my eyes takes effort. I see her being furiously rubbed with towels under a warmer. The baby doesn't cry, then does. Her hands are balled in fists. She weighs nearly nine pounds. She looks like a tiny, angry model of my father and there is a semicircular bruise on her cheek from the forceps. Scott is crying. The doula is taking pictures. It is just after four thirty in the afternoon, a mere sixteen hours after the whole thing began.

I am shivering again, violently this time, and freezing. No one is concerned. All eyes are on the baby, except mine, which are closed. The placenta is delivered and I am stitched up, which I don't feel. The baby is being whisked down to the NICU because her lungs sound odd, a side effect of all the time she spent locked in my pelvis. But she is here, finally. I relax. Birth is always the hardest part. It can only be downhill from here.

All narratives break down.

After the birth, life got blurry. For the myopic like me, an analogy: it was like walking around without your corrective lenses, where everything—from oncoming cars to the living room sofa—is reduced to nice benign blobs of color, which can't hurt you because they don't have sharp edges. Sounds become squishy, too. Speaking voices ape Charlie Brown's parents, if Chuck's folks were trapped in a coal mine. Food loses its taste, simply because you can't tell if that brown fuzzy thing is chicken or beef or bread. It feels safe, this soft world. It's like living in Teletubby land while being gently stoned. But there are still sharp dragons out there ready to bite and they can sneak up before you spot them.

For those with perfect vision, whom I curse, an illustrative story, plucked from the first fourteen days that I was home postbirth:

The first big baby-free journey I made was to my

boss's wedding in July. I'm sure it was a beautiful event, but I don't remember most of it, a faux pas that will probably land me in wedding-guest purgatory. The pageantry floated past this guest. I'm not certain that I ever gave them a gift. Miss Manners would be so disappointed.

All that led up to the bride's processional is fairly clear. I had rummaged through my closet like a rat through a Dumpster, desperately trying to find some summery, dressy outfit to fit my new, deflated frame. None of my prepreggers clothes fit, but I tried them on anyway, which only made me feel crappier about my new form. After sifting through a dozen years of poor fashion choices, I got to the end of the rod, where all of the fat clothes lived. From there I made my choice, an elastic-waist skirt I hadn't worn since high school and a peach T-shirt covered in thread pills.

I was crying, of course, but also oozing other bodily fluids. Baby books warn you about this panoply of liquid that a new mother's body produces, but they fail to convey the reality. My skin was constantly covered in a thin sheen of perspiration, partly because it was a humid Tennessee summer and partly because this is how one's body gets rid of all the fluid it retained during the third trimester. Things were funkier below what used to be my waist. A lingering issue from the marathon of pushing was that my bladder nerves were no longer communicating with my brain. Not only would I sneeze and pee, but I could walk and pee or climb stairs and pee or just sit quietly and pee. Then, of course, is what is politely called lochia, which is the flood of gook that flows out of your newly contracted uterus and is contained only by the enormous sanitary napkins that my mother's generation swore by. Luckily, they also absorbed all the urine. I did, however, have that not-so-fresh feeling.

I wasn't sure that I could contain all of the liquid long enough to make it out of the house and into the car, much less through a whole wedding. The wisest course of action seemed to be to stay inside my quiet little house where I would embarrass myself only in front of my husband (who, since he hadn't decided to run like a track star during labor, was probably going to stick around for a bit). Other people would be at the wedding, people who saw me as a mostly sane, professional adult, rather than a flabby bag that leaked the whole band—blood, sweat, and tears. My cover would be blown and there would be no cramming this shameful damp genie back into its bottle. I decided to not go and walked out to the kitchen to inform Scott of this. "Go," he said. "It'll do you good."

"But . . ." I said.

"Go," he said. Beneath his easygoing exterior lies an easygoing core. But occupying a very small corner of that core is a chunk of annealed iron, which I could see as I gathered up my cop-outs with the car keys.

The wedding was held on the grounds of a historic mansion in the heart of the city. Most of the midsummer mugginess had left for the day and, although it was warm, it wasn't oppressive. It was the kind of day that makes you fall a little bit in love with Knoxville, with its clear skies and blooming flowers and well-dressed company—almost like a commercial for a fabric softener. Women with carefully arranged hair wore strapless floral dresses from Talbots or Dillards; their men were in light-colored suits or chinos and dress shirts. A ragtag clump of the artistically attired and coiffed, which was pretty much all of my coworkers and friends, gathered on one side to gossip and observe.

We were outside, in white chairs. There were white tents. Everyone told me I looked just great for having just had a baby. I knew the truth, of course, but the lies were well intentioned and appreciated.

"How was it?" asked J, a woman about the same age as me who I suspected was considering taking the plunge.

"Long," I said, "but fine." I smiled. I couldn't tell her the truth, about the pain and the blood. It's like getting the best Christmas gift ever, but Santa decided to kick the crap out of you before you unwrapped it. No one wants to know the truth.

The ceremony started and I left. Not physically, of course; that would have been rude. My damp rear stayed there in my folding chair, wedged between two people who used to know me before I gave birth. But the rest of me checked out. It wasn't like when I'd stop paying attention in class or that otherworldly feeling right before falling asleep. I would like to say that it was like a movie, where I hovered about the proceedings in soft focus and a long-flowing gown but my life isn't that poetic. Really, it was as if some giant hand turned down the volume. Everything—from sound to color to temperature—flattened into comfortable, harmless blobs, which moved around in pretty and inscrutable ways.

Then the ceremony ended. The world refocused when I noticed those around me standing up. There was chitchat. One guest, whose girlfriend is a midwife, told me the story of a baby she delivered who was born in its amniotic sac. Someone related the tale of how Diane is faring with her newborn, who was the same age as mine. She'd had to quit breastfeeding because she had ruptured sucking blisters on her nipples and the baby had gotten a belly full of blood. The gossipers are worried about her, myself included, because I am a hypocrite. Diane just seemed so manic, so over the top with glee about everything. Diane never seemed to complain about anything that new moms complain about. And there are rumors that she's already lost all of her baby weight, which can't be healthy. I can feel the judgments being weighed.

Talking to other adults is exhausting. Finding words—any words, much less those that made sense—is brutal. Whole pages were missing from my mental dictionary and my fingers would stumble through the book trying to piece together sentences without a full component of needed parts.

It is hard not to grab people I know by the shoulders and scream at them to help me. But my cheap dramatics would have detracted from my boss and his new wife's special day. And I'd had my special day, hadn't I, where I got to experience the joy and wonder of childbirth? Asking for another felt greedy.

Exhausted, I walk back to my car, where I catch some of my coworkers drinking bourbon and smoking home-grown dope on the tailgate of a pickup truck. They look like tropical birds, all bright colors and movement, and glimpses of giggling, happy (if chemically enhanced) life bring on more tears. I can't remember what it was like to feel that light.

I don't want to go home and deal with the baby, who is nothing but nine pounds of need. But I don't want to stay. It was too happy, too shrill, too real. I don't fit anymore. And my arm is tired from holding up my damn mask, the one that makes it look like I am okay.

*   *   *

The above anecdote helps explain that I don't remember a lot of what happened during the seventy-two hours I was allowed to stay in the hospital after labor. Mostly I stared off into space, I think, while trying to wrap my mind around all that had happened, a condition that would continue to haunt me for months. Swaddled like a burrito in a portable isolet, the baby came and went, wheeled about by nurses. The baby stared off into space most of the time, too, and I imagine she was also trying to wrap her mind around what had just happened.

There are clear spots. After my OB had done the requisite stitching of my nether regions—I found it disturbing that she wouldn't tell me how many stitches she put in my tender flesh—the baby came back from having her first X-ray, my violent shivers wound down, and the room slowly cleared out. The nurse who had stuck with me through the whole endless process changed my sheets and replaced the thick absorbent pads under my bottom. An orderly pushed around a mop, then left. The doula showed me the basics of nursing and we roused the baby enough to waggle my nipple at her. She looked at us like we were absolute loons and promptly dropped back to sleep in my arms. My God, she was cute. My husband beamed at us or, perhaps, at my bared breast.

The baby didn't have a name yet. Two had topped our list of potentials and we were divided over which one it would be. My secret plan had been to force the Hub into my favorite after the baby arrived, when I could play the guilt card. But once I saw her, I knew that his favorite—the name that we had stumbled upon one night while driving home from a Christmas party—was the right one. "Madeline?" he asked. It was our interpretation of my paternal great-grandmother's name, the matriarch Mama

Lane. Now it would also be my daughter's name. It's a good one, I think, and suits her well.

Once that was resolved and all of the paperwork filled in, it was as if one of the nurses had slipped me a mickey. Even if Johnny Depp had stumbled into the room wearing nothing but his tattoos and a smile, I couldn't have stayed awake.

Ten minutes later my eyes popped open, responding to the racket my belly was sending out. My mom swooped in to examine her granddaughter and, I suppose, daughter. "What took so long?" she asked. I couldn't tell her. Clever, new-mother mental sprites had already started to work their magic, blotting out the memory of the last twenty-four hours with a giddy rush of adrenaline. I could have scaled the outside of the maternity ward, if only my legs were working again after so many hours of painkillers. My skin seemed to hum, like sparks of static would zap the next person who touched me. I was alive—so alive my teeth were grinding—and had the most wonderful baby anyone has ever had ever.

With the manic glee came brutal hunger. My mom set out for the cafeteria. A nurse promised to scare up a dinner tray. Scott started to make the requisite calls while I gnawed on a Luna bar, which normally calls to mind chewy tree bark but, at that moment, tasted like an exotically spiced nugget of pure joy. I wanted more. More! Slices of rare beef nestled next to mashed potatoes, blanketed by a rich brown gravy. A bowl of chili, with heaps of Cheddar cheese and sour cream. A fat, juicy cheeseburger with fat slices of onion and crisp lettuce, gently caressed by beer-battered onion rings. Speaking of—I wanted a beer, an indulgence I'd not known for the last nine months. I would go fetch it myself, once I could figure out how to stand up without the disturbing sensation of my internal organs tumbling down to my toes.

My mom returned with a Styrofoam container of Jell-O.

Here's the thing—as much as I harp on my mother's shortcomings, this isn't one of them. Since I had called out to her to just "bring back anything," I can't bitch too much, which doesn't stop me most of the time. Her heart was in the right place. Jell-O was her standard panacea for whatever might ail you. Some of my fondest memories are staying home sick from school, wrapped up in an afghan on the sofa while watching daytime TV and slurping cherry Jell-O off a teaspoon. But, right now, I needed more.

I wolfed down the Jell-O and started pondering walking down to the cafeteria my own damn self when a plate full of fried chicken arrived, courtesy of the nursing staff. Without qualifications, it is the best fried chicken I have ever eaten. Note that I didn't claim it was merely the best hospital food I have eaten. This particular dish tops my list of the all-time most amazingly satisfying meals I have ever had.

After ogling the new baby a bit longer, Mom left. The three of us were alone together, for the first time.

"Well done, you," Scott said as he kissed me and sat on my bed. The baby was next to us. We held hands and gazed at her, while a violent summer thunderstorm crashed outside. Water poured down the windows, as if we were in our car and going through the car wash. Next would come the hot wax.

Actually, next was a blackout. It was early evening— still enough light to see by but still kinda dark. When the lights went out, so did the background noises of ticks and beeps and voices, the ubiquitous maternity ward mood music. We just continued to sit there, awestruck by almost nine pounds of baby in the hushed, dark room. She slept. We watched. I couldn't stop marveling at her hands, the two tiny fists clenched under her chin. They were mind-blowing. My body knew how to make perfect little hands, complete with tiny fingernails and adorable thumbs. I had no idea I could work such magic. It was all I could do to not unwrap her feet, with their caper-sized toes, which begged to be nibbled on. I contented myself with reaching over to brush my fingers across the top of her head, tickling the brown fuzz that coated her big, round melon of a skull. Her left cheek was marred with a bright red, U-shaped bruise, where the forceps had been clamped. Even the bruise was beautiful. I had been warned that newborns are not the most attractive of critters with their pointy heads and chickenlike scrawniness. But Madeline was more magnetic than the North Pole. In this silent twilight, time passed.

More haziness ensues. Eventually, I drift off to sleep. The baby is taken to the Maternity Ward's holding pen. While it is tempting to keep her with us all night, good sense prevails. If she were in the room, I'd never sleep, rousing at every single gurgle, convinced she was about to perish. The drugs are wearing off, finally, and every piece of anatomy south of my collarbones is starting to realize that it has been part of a bloody uprising. There are protests. The peasants are hollering recriminations and waving torches. Sleep is the only thing that will quell the coming revolution.

During the night's wee hours, a nurse wheels in the baby. The mewling emerging from her box is grating.

"I don't want to wake you but she's starving," the nurse says.

I rouse myself and pluck out a breast, careful to make sure it's not the same one that was last offered. The La Leche League's handbook has been my bedtime reading for the last four weeks and I am schooled on how one does this lactating thing. Milk will flow from my body like those dancing fountains in Vegas.

The baby is purple with rage. Gone is blissed-out angel, replaced by vigorous desperation.

We tease her mouth into a big O and jam my nipple in. The baby gives a suck. Her big blue eyes glare at us, easily transmitting her thoughts, which run along the lines of "What the hell am I supposed to do with this?"

The nurse unlatches the babe and flattens my breast as if she were taking a mammogram. The infant is reattached. Still the same glare.

This goes on. The nurse squishing, the baby resisting, and me helpless. I don't know how the species has survived this long, given how difficult this breastfeeding is. Unflappable, this nurse pulls out a needleless syringe that is as big around as my thumb. "Your nipples aren't popping out," she tells me. It's not an accusation, but a statement of fact. My recalcitrant nipple is placed under the open end of the syringe and coaxed erect with the suction. (It sounds much more erotic than it was. Trust me.) With great haste—lest the little bugger should again vanish—my child is attached to it. She sucks a bit, which I really don't feel, then drops off to sleep. We all assume that she's getting what she needs.

Every couple of hours, a new nurse, the baby, and I would repeat this exercise with the suction and the nipple. I am given hard plastic shells, which sort of look like the two halves of a yo-yo, to wear on the ends of my breasts in order to encourage more productive nipple action. With my top on, I am indistinguishible from Madonna during her Gaultier/cone-shaped tits phase. Unfortunately, the similarities end when you look away from my chest.

More blurriness ensues. My mom visits, gives the baby stuffed animals, and leaves. Scott comes and goes. He brings food (barring that fried-chicken feast, the hospital food is about as bad as expected) and cards and flowers. I take my first shower and, apart from all of the gore running down the inside of my legs, I feel like a new woman. I also discover the joy of the sitz bath, something that I'd previously thought was only in the purview of old Jewish men. If you take nothing else away from this cautionary tale, remember only this: the sitz bath rocks. Succumb to the sitz bath.

The morning of the second day—the day of my forced release from the Maternity Ward—my OB drops in for her last visit. The baby is on the bed in front of me, swaddled up tightly. I am staring down at her and bawling. Big tear stains darken the sheets around her. I've not been myself the past couple of days. It is safe to say that I am not entirely sure now what the definition of *myself* is.

My doctor asks what is wrong.

"She's just so beautiful," I sob. I don't finish the thought, however. The rest of it runs something like "and I don't have any idea how a sack of shit like me could have made something so gorgeous." Had I kept talking, I probably could have saved everyone a lot of trouble and been wheeled directly from my maternity bed to a psych bed. Ah, hindsight.

While I continue to weep, she listens to my heart and lungs and belly, then pronounces me physically well enough to go home. The crying chalked up to run-of-the-mill baby blues, I am cautioned to call if it keeps up for more than a couple weeks. With that, she leaves and I am free to go.

The baby, however, isn't. After I get the tears under control, I notice that her coloring seems funky. Her porcelain skin is taking on an orangey glow, which I chalk up to the sunlight that we were finally seeing after days of rain. I start packing up two days' worth of flowers and stuffed animals. I notice that I haven't worn my new soft green floral pajamas, which I'd bought because they looked so clean and motherly, perfect for my days in the hospital. A pediatrician breezes in and whisks the baby away. A bit later, she comes back.

"I'm going to let you go," she tells us, "but you'll have to come to the office tomorrow so that we can keep an eye on the jaundice."

The penny drops. The baby's big pumpkin head is orange from jaundice, not from the lighting. While the numbers on her blood test nudge the upper limit of what is reasonable, the pediatrician decides we are an acceptable risk and lets us take the baby home. Paperwork is signed, including a document that certifies that we have a clean water supply. Ah, Tennessee. We load her into the car seat, which is a fumbly process full of false starts and blind corners. Scott and I are slightly concerned that we haven't the slightest clue what we're doing, but are reasonably certain that we can handle anything. We'd made it this far in life, after all. How tricky can a baby be?

4

Most roads in the eastern United States lead to Knoxville. Literally. Imagine Knoxville as the great big filter that separates North from South, both metaphorically and geographically. It is where I-40 and I-75 physically intersect in a mess of an interchange that makes even brave men weep. From the city, you can get almost anywhere in the Southeast with little effort. Atlanta is close. Nashville is closer. Asheville is closer still. The beach is a sixish-hour drive. The Great Smoky Mountains are less than forty-five minutes from the heart of downtown. In many ways, it is the ideal location, close to bigger cities and wide-open spaces without the hassles of either.

Wherever you are, you can always find someone who knows Knoxville. A woman in my yoga class in a wee town in New York went to grad school at the University of Tennessee in Knoxville and knows some of the theater folk I used to hang with. When I was in London, I met a cabbie who had a sister who had recently left Knoxville for Central Florida. When I lived in Austin and was writing for the *Chronicle*, I knew a fellow scribe only through e-mail, but he had grown up in Knoxville—and I met him in person only after I moved there myself. I suspect that even in farthest Mongolia you could find someone who knows what it means when you say, "Go, Vols."

Contrary to popular belief, Knoxville is not the home of Fort Knox, which is actually in Kentucky. Knoxville was, however, the site of the 1982 World's Fair—a tidbit of information that never fails to surprise the uninitiated. The fair left in its wake a huge erection called the Sunsphere, which resembles a big, golden golf ball on a dark green tee, and a park, which no one knew what to do with until the turn of the most recent century. Thanks to the Sunsphere, Knoxville has also been immortalized in an episode of *The Simpsons*, when Bart and his buddies traveled to town to discover that the entire structure was full of wigs. For the record, it isn't, but that doesn't stop most Knoxvillians from dreaming that it is, because it would be much cooler that way.

It is fitting that Knoxville was home to a World's Fair that most outsiders can't recall. This Appalachian jewel has always been the most neglected of Tennessee's major cities, which are represented on the state flag with three white stars. Memphis is known for the blues and barbecue. Nashville is known for the country music industry and southern charm. Knoxville, well, Knoxville has bluegrass, the bastard child of American music. Save for April when the dogwoods are in bloom, the city lacks any real visual charm with which to woo outsiders. There is no regional cuisine to speak of, either, and most of the city's "special" dishes—like pulled pork sandwiches and chowchow and banana pudding—can be found on almost any menu in the region. Most of the folks who grew up there seem deeply apologetic about their native town. A New York writer once called Knoxville a "scruffy little city," nomenclature that still works, even though the city's political honchos would have you believe otherwise. According to the boosters, Knoxville is the jewel of the southern Appalachians, a Mecca that is rivaled only by Atlanta when it comes to business brilliance, family friendliness, and liberal (but not too liberal, like where gays and atheists are tolerated) thought. The truth is that Knoxville is like any other town its size, full of contradictions and strip malls.

Image-conscious corporations like Scripps Howard's cable channels—HGTV, the Food Network, the DIY Network, and Fine Living—are based in shiny offices on the city's western fringe. As a result, a dozen TV production houses dot the landscape like mushrooms after a rain. At almost any large gathering, you can find at least one person who has wound up on national TV via a Knoxville-based production. Even the Hub and I have had our fifteen minutes, on the DIY network. The show was called *To the Rescue* and featured a talent staff of home-improvement experts who swoop in to fix a seriously botched project. Our master bedroom was tapped because (a) it is the definition of botched and (b) the network people liked the fact that we don't have thick regional accents, which I'm told don't play well on Scripps networks.

Other industries dot the city as well. TVA, the alphabet administration that controls most of the power in the Southeast, has two monoliths in the heart of downtown, near the home of Kimberly-Clark. Most major corporations settle there because it is near everything but doesn't have all of the hassles and high costs of big-city business. Plus, Knoxville is in a right-to-work state (read: almost no pesky unions to speak of) and has no state income tax. Life in Knoxville is cheap and more or less easy. The rent on our first apartment—a decent, huge place with an amazing view of the mountains—was exactly the same as on our crappy little shoebox in Austin that had a stunning view of the back of a Walgreens. In Manhattan, the same amount of scratch would get us three square feet of sidewalk, but only if we were willing to sublet from the Korean grocery owner whose business it fronts.

Of course, if you are not a Southern Baptist or want to send your kids to a decent school, your day-to-day existence is a bit more tedious in this city on the Tennessee River. Most of my friends in Knoxville were from someplace else, which I knew on meeting them because their first question wasn't, "Which church do y'all go to?" With the natives, that question is a trap. Answer wrong and you'll find yourself shunned or, worse yet, visited by well-dressed matrons who will guilt you to their parish one Sunday morning, wooing you with potato salad and sweet tea. If you are not careful, you'll be dunked in the river for good measure.

Knoxville, like most of Tennessee, never quite cottoned to the idea of providing a decent public education to all of the state's young, regardless of their parents' color or marital or income status. Again, there is no state income tax—a point of pride, in fact, for all of the Tennesseeans who are bad at math, which is most of them, since the schools suck so badly. The infrastructure for schools and other social services is only one small step above Bangalore's. If your family has money, you'll make it through okay because you'll be shipped off to a fairly white, fairly affluent private school where you'll meet only other kids whose backgrounds are just like yours. Public school is home to the kids whose parents work for a living. While most cities have this problem, the class stratification is stronger here than anyplace else I've lived. You always know where you fall in the city's social strata and you are never allowed to forget it.

Not being a native and, at the time, not having any offspring, I didn't much care about the schools or what others believed about my social class. I was one of those artsy people fresh in from Austin, a city that was in the middle of being strip-mined by Hollywood and the recording industry for all of its cool, indy cred. The now-Hub but then-boyfriend and I had wound up in Austin purely by chance. He'd been accepted to grad school at the University of Texas and I didn't really have anything else planned for my postgraduation life. After four years of working toward a theater degree, I was slowly starting to realize that I wasn't cut out for a life on the stage—but I also had no idea what else I would do. So, I moved to Austin with a guy and later married him. My feminist foremothers would be appalled. My parents certainly were, convinced that I would be wasting my life in, of all places, Texas, miles and miles and miles away from green mountains, tall trees, and decent Italian food.

I cried for the first month we lived in the Lone Star State, convinced that I'd made a huge mistake. We moved there in August of a year when it didn't rain all summer, which spanned from April to October. The heat was a third person living in our cramped apartment, where we slept on the floor because we didn't own a bed. Once school started, I never saw the man I'd moved down with. Leaving the apartment was a challenge, both because of the heat and the dicey neighborhood, where a needle truck patrolled the streets and always had a line of junkies streaming behind it. I would leave just long enough to go to my crappy job at a Crate and Barrel–esque shop in the mall, then come home and cry some more. Some days, I wouldn't make it home before the tears started. In the parking lot, they'd hit the pavement and evaporate as the heat stole every last drop of moisture.

About the time I was convinced I was going to cover all of the windows with aluminum foil to block out the oppressive sunlight, it rained, a glorious downpour complete with thunder and lightning and floods. When it started at 2 a.m., we poked our heads out of the bedroom window and could see our neighbors dancing in the streets. A few days later, I quit my job and found one at a bookstore within walking distance of our squalid place. Life improved. About three years into our Austin sojourn, I figured out that I like writing better than anything else and went to UT to pick up a second degree.

After five years there, I was ready to leave. Austin is a great place to live, as long as you don't mind the constant heat and oppressive hipsters. But it was time for me to go. I've never even been a good fake Texan and am completely unable to embrace the expansiveness that is their birthright. There's too much sun and too much sky and too much space. Give me a good narrow mountain holler any day.

Scott was done with grad school and had his first teaching gig two thousand miles away near Philadelphia. I was hanging out in Austin for a few months to finish up my degree, then I would either join him or, if the market was willing, find my own job and he would join me. Our working theory was that, since I had followed him to Texas, he would follow me now. The day he left, I started to cry again, the same unstoppable sobbing that had plagued me when we'd first moved down. Part of it was the knowledge that I'd truly be alone for months on end, for the first time in my adult life. But most of it was the knowledge that I'd have to take a plane to visit him or, worse yet, ride in a car for more than an hour.

Sometime during the last decade or so, my mild fear of flying had turned into a full-blown terror of any kind of lengthy trip in any kind of conveyance. I'd spend nights wide awake, hearing planes fly overhead—our Austin apartment was on the airport's approach path—or dreaming of ways they'd crash. I could barely drive the five miles from my bedroom to the campus without picturing my car in a mangled heap, with my limbs splayed and bloodied out the open window. The temptation just to close my eyes behind the wheel and let the accident come was undeniable. It whispered to me, like a lover with a new come-on and sex toy.

After one particularly gruesome drive to campus, I delivered myself to the health center, which promptly delivered me to a student shrink. She agreed to take me on gratis as long as I let her use me as a case study for her final course work. Somewhere, deep in the bowels of UT's Psych Department, I am the secret star of a dissertation. This amuses me.

My shrink decided that I needed meds, which I fought against with every last fiber of my pathetic being, convinced that they'd turn me into a happy little zombie who'd never write another word. But wouldn't it be nice, she'd ask, to not feel like death was waiting at every turn? Yes, I'd say, but that's what gives me my edge. Without that, I'm boring. And one day, on the way to an appointment with her, I stepped out into traffic with a reckless disregard for where the cars were. I came within inches of a trip to the ER (or worse) and scared myself so badly that I was sobbing and shaking and ranting the rest of the way to her office. I agreed to take the damn drugs, which made me dizzy and queasy and sleepy and a couple of other dwarves. Yet, within a week or so, I could focus on something besides my death. I finished my classwork, freelanced my fingers to the bone, and found a real editing gig in Knoxville for the weekly paper. Thanks to the pharmaceutical industry, I was able to take a plane to that interview and back without clutching at the flight attendants like a toddler grabbing at candy.

Almost to a person, everyone I met during my first weeks in Knoxville apologized for it not being as hip as Austin. No matter how many times I explained that if I'd loved Austin's hipness so much, I would have stayed there, everyone felt compelled to provide condolences for their scruffy town. Then, they'd launch into a spiel about how great Knoxville is, how friendly the folks are, and how gorgeous the mountains can be. You could get whiplash from the quick turn.

The schizophrenia about the city is telling something best illustrated by the writers that Knoxville has turned out. James Agee grew up in Fort Sanders, the neighborhood that fronts the university. His Pulitzer prize–winning "A Death in the Family" gently and poetically examines all of the city's contradictions—between black and white, rich and poor—while nudging at larger issues about families and death. Frances Hodgson Burnett was British born but Knoxville bred and her *The Secret Garden* could be pictured easily in one of the city's tonier districts. But for each quiet tale told by elegant writers, there is a Cormac McCarthy, whose dark, violent southern Gothic tales like *Suttree* and *Blood Meridian* come the

closest to getting at the heart of Knoxville. While Mc-
Carthy quit the place in the early 1970s, you can still feel
the echoes of East Tennessee in his more brooding pas-
sages. The weird band of beer drinkers I used to hang
with in town annually reenacts scenes from *Suttree*, turning it into a drunken stagger to all of the grimy places
McCarthy vividly depicts. A watermelon in lingerie is
given a prominent place on the bar of the last stop, a
homage to one of the book's more colorful characters
who happens to enjoy carnal knowledge with these ripe
melons on slow summer days.

Knoxville is also known for the musicians who died
after stops there. Rachmaninoff played his last recital in
Knoxville in 1943, then died of cancer. Hank Williams's
last night on this earth was spent being driven around
greater Knoxville by his chauffeur, who may or may not
have realized that his charge had OD'd in the backseat.
Some day, I want to write a play called *Driving Mr.
Williams*. There will be heartbreaking ballads and lots of
morphine.

On a good night, you can almost feel all of these
ghosts lingering along the center city's streets, whispering
ideas to you as you pass. A dark, creative spirit is nearly
tangible when you get down by the river, which has in-
spired many a bluegrass ballad about drowning. For that
reason, Knoxville always pulls part of you back, once
you've gotten to know her. It's not the corporate office
blocks or the shiny new convention center, which was
sold to the city's movers and shakers like so much snake
oil. It's the city's grimy, lovable heart that beats dark po-
etry to those who can hear it thumping. To quote
Knoxville-based songwriter Scott Miller, who has spent
most of his career capturing the town's spirit:

Hank Williams and James Agee hiding back in the
    hills
A bottle full of whiskey and some sleeping pills
Hank tells Jimmy, "If you write me a book,
I'll write you a ditty with a real mean hook
Called 'You Can't Shake Knoxville.'"

And you can't shake it, no matter how far you run, which makes it just like other parts of Appalachia. Unlike Parkersburg, Knoxville makes a point of playing up its hillbilly character. It's a defense mechanism, making fun of itself in a preemptive strike so that you won't feel badly about making fun of it as well. Just down the road from the city is the region's true spiritual center, where Dolly Parton's theme park and tacky-ass Gatlinburg meet in an unholy amalgam of outlet shops, Thomas Kincaid paintings, tattoo parlors, and "family entertainment." Dollywood itself continually winks at you, as if the park itself knows how branded the "hillbilly experience" has become. The Aunt Granny's eatery is a must-visit on the park's grounds, where you can get fried chicken, greens, and biscuits while pondering what shape a family's tree must be in to have an Aunt Granny. Down the road a spell is Christus Gardens, a small theme "experience" devoted to dioramas about the life of Christ. You can even buy a Christus shot glass in the gift shop, if you are so inclined. On any given Saturday, you can stroll the streets and see what most Americans—the folks whose opinions aren't important because they live in a fly-over state and have mullets—look like, WWE T-shirts and all. It's not pretty, but that doesn't make it any less true.

But what do I know? I'm a card-carrying member of the liberal elite. I know the secret handshake and everything. Still and all, natives of Knoxville adopt an outlaw swagger and throw off a vibe from a Steve Earle song populated by moonshine runners and petty thieves. This covers up a deeper insecurity about feeling unworthy because they grew up in the hills, surrounded by kinfolk and Bibles.

It's all of a piece, this place. You can drive from Pittsburgh to Parkersburg to Knoxville and feel you haven't really changed locations. While the size of the cities changes (and Pittsburgh's culture has also been shaped by its thriving immigrant culture that neither Knoxville nor Parkersburg can claim), their spirits are the same. In any restaurant, you can hear nearly identical harsh accents, pocked with exclamations of "yinz," the Appalachian equivalent of "y'all." Start a conversation about the town's history, and you'll stumble into a discourse on how they didn't pick a side during the Civil War and how the local economy has always been based on small, nonplantation farms and outside industries like steel and coal and decades of extraordinary poverty. The mountains never really change, cutting across the landscape like rugs bunched up on hardwood floors. As you drive farther south, they simply get greener. And the people, once you get to know them, will always tell you that the place they grew up in makes them feel somehow "less-than," as if all that America stands for doesn't apply to them.

For outsiders, Knoxville is a place you end up when you're not paying enough attention. I wound up there because it was just time for me to get out of Austin and find a real job. Once I got to Knoxville, it was hard to leave. The city's low self-esteem meshed ideally with my own personality quirks. I never felt hip enough in Austin. I didn't smoke enough weed or go to the right shows or geek out in the cool bookstores. But in Knoxville, where any vaguely artsy person is immediately granted outsider cachet, I fit right in. While some far "out-eclecticked" me, I found a comfortable middle ground where I didn't have to work too hard to keep up with the city's avant-garde.

For my cousin Joan, Knoxville—technically Halls, a bedroom community just outside of the city proper—was the ideal spot to retreat from the world at large. She found herself there because of her husband, who had a nebulous-insurance industry job that I've never really been able to grok and was transferred every few years. Our Tennessee tenures didn't overlap. Her Halls stint preceded my Knoxville time by two years. The first year I was in Knoxville, she was living just outside of Nashville, again because of her husband's work-related promotion. Still, it was the closest I'd lived to my mother's side of the family since forever, and it was nice to be able to drive out to her place just after Christmas and see people I'm related to.

By her own account, Joan loved Halls. Everything anyone could ever need was there—including a Wal-Mart and a variety of fast food—and you never had to drive to the city proper. It was a nice, safe place to raise her kids, who were just at the age when they get into all-American activities like cheerleading and softball. But Halls wasn't the Eden Joan had thought. Even the most quaint town has its secrets. In 1994, Halls was the site of a good old southern tradition, a cross burning, which took place on the lawn of one Dennis Willis, a black man. Willis and his wife have three kids, two of whom were too young at the time to understand the threat. The twelve-year-old, however, was distraught. The local church members, of course, denounced the act and the Willis family was reportedly heartened by the outpouring of support. Still, the hand-wringing didn't change the fact that parts of Tennessee harbored hate groups, which jumped into the fray and papered the neighborhood with antiblack literature. The Willises were continually harassed by cowards who'd leave threats on their doorstep under cover of night. The FBI was called in but, ten years later, the case is still unsolved and the Willises have moved. But this wasn't the last episode in the area. In 2001, a cross was burned on the front lawn of Roland Dykes, nearby Newport's first black mayor.

Like towns, families have their hidden shames, too. On the surface, Joan and her brood seemed fairly content. Big gatherings were common and full of laughter. As a writer, I'm supposed to set up the fall at this point, where I point to all of the outward trappings of success like a big house and healthy, smart kids. I find it oddly exhausting to paint the picture for you, because I know how it ended. Suffice to say, Joan's family was exactly what you'd expect for the upwardly mobile middle class. And, yet, something eroded the foundation.

If you ask Joan's former husband, no doubt he'd claim it was her fault that he sought refuge in the arms of his young French coworker, who recently bore his third child. You'd have to ask him yourself, though. After so many years of being an integral, trusted part of the family, he now makes me spit when his name is mentioned because of his betrayal of my cousin. I mean, if you're going to leave, at least try to be original about it. But dumping your wife of many years for a pretty young thing is just so clichéd. Why not break the mold and leave so that you can join the circus to find your inner clown? Or travel to the forests of Oregon to find Bigfoot? We all make choices, but some are just so very predictable.

Anyway, his wife couldn't provide him with comfort because she was clinically depressed and taking meds for it. Joan, the cousin who I always thought was the sanest of us all (oddly, she thought the same thing about me), spent years struggling with depression. And, as a nurse, she's also confessed that she's spent time on both sides of the Psych Ward's doors.

Her ex-husband, of course, used this against her in the divorce proceedings. According to Joan, "He told the court I was dangerous and got custody of my teenagers for a couple of years. Talk about total agony! Of course, ninety-nine percent of it was not true, but he used it and since most people are uneducated about the mentally ill, they fear us. People think they don't know any mentally ill people, when really we are everywhere. Doctors, neighbors, coworkers, rich, poor. But let's face it, you have to keep your diagnosis a secret from people until after they realize how sane and stable you are. God forbid they catch you at a fragile moment. How ironic, huh?

"There have been times well-meaning people have seen me in my full-blown state of illness and said, 'Hey, just walk it off,' 'Cheer up' and 'Count your blessings.' Would you tell a person with muscular dystrophy to 'walk it off'? It's not her fault. Don't get me wrong—I don't flaunt it or use it as a crutch, either, but there's a happy medium in there somewhere."

Joan's story takes an upward turn. She has remarried. Her new husband is, incidentally, bipolar. And, as it turns out, so is her seventeen-year-old daughter, who now lives with her. Everyone is on top of his or her own illness, most of the time. This can always change—such is the nature of life and brain chemistry—but everyone is doing quite well, thank you very much.

For each heartwarming family story, however, there is one that is less so. Joan is the only cousin who can remember our uncle Bill, the youngest child of the W. C. Tebay line and the only male. Joan was six when he shot himself in 1970, old enough to feel the loss. I wasn't even a glimmer in my parents' eyes at that point and my cousin Julie, Joan's sister, may have been just implanting herself in Linda's womb.

I know Bill only from some faded pictures in my mom's albums and a glove box full of his badges, pins, and aviator shades stashed in a hope chest. The photos show a sunny, blond teen with piercing brown eyes, the look of a football hero likely to snare the heart of any girl. He had the personality to match, a great guy, always the life of the party. Cheerful and productive, my aunt Linda says, just happy-go-lucky. Always. He was drafted and sent to Vietnam in 1968, which isn't an unusual American story. When he came back a year later, he had changed. He was withdrawn, almost afraid. He was different.

No one came back from Vietnam with a skip in his step and spring in his heart. Like all wars, it was brutal and inhumane. The boys who went didn't come back the same. Only foolish people would expect that.

The Army, however, is generally not foolish. When he returned to the base from his leave, they sent him home with a prescription for psychoactive drugs because he needed more time to get his head together. Apparently, they wanted him to be less insane before they sent him back to the front to commit insane acts.

The story starts to get muddled at this point. My aunt seems to have the clearest memory of it, since she was the one who still lived near their father and Bill in Parkersburg. "Somewhere in there, he ended up at Snooks's house and, then, Fort Jackson," she says. "I don't remember whether he had transferred there or whether he had gone on his own. But he ended up there in a manic state and they put him in for psychiatric counseling. Then they sent him home somewhere around Christmas. He was on medication. He still was just not happy, not himself. He was like a different person.

"After every Christmas, Dad and Marguerite [his second wife, whom he married three years after Nell's death] would go to Marathon, Florida. They'd stay for several weeks. So Bill went with them. When he left them that year, he was to fly from Miami straight to the base. He didn't. He flew to Parkersburg. One night I went to my door and there he was. I said 'Come on in' and he stayed with us that night. Then the next day he wanted to go over to Dad's [empty] house. So he did.

"The next night, he didn't want to go back to the base. He said he didn't want to go back. Steve [Linda's then-husband] talked to him and he kept saying, 'You know, you don't have but six or eight months left. Once you go back, you don't have much longer. Just stick it out and you'll be all right.'

"Bill called sometime that morning. It had snowed and the Superbowl was that day—the Jets, because I remember Joe Namath was playing. Bill called and I said, 'Are you going to come over and watch the game? I'm making some pancakes and eggs. Why don't you come over?' He said 'I don't want to come there. I don't want to go out in the snow. I don't even know if the car will start.

Why don't you have Steve come over here?' And I said, 'Well, okay. Steve'll come over and I'll come over later.' Bill knew that Steve was coming. That's when he did it. Steve found him.

"I swear, from that day until Julie got sick and I heard the audiotape of Kay Redfield Jamison's *An Unquiet Mind*, I did not understand. I didn't understand why he did that. I know it was a mental condition, but for all those years, what I always thought—and what your mom, Snooks, and I had talked about—we thought maybe he had gone to Vietnam and like many of the other people, had taken LSD or something that caused mental problems—that's what we thought had caused all of this. That's what had thrown him into doing weird things and depression. It didn't seem important because, I mean, why dwell on any negatives? Why dwell on anything like that if it's not important. And until Julie got sick, it just didn't seem that important.

"Once I heard that tape and I remembered that Mother's aunt had raised her and it was said that Mother's mother was an alcoholic—you know, not much was said about it—I just put two and two together. After reading *An Unquiet Mind* and looking back in my own family, I came to the realization that Bill's suicide was triggered by his bipolar disorder—the depression side of the bipolar disorder. I realized how this genetic chemical imbalance, which usually begins in the early to mid-twenties, caused him to end his life. Until then, I could not understand why my brother, who was so wonderful and had so much for which to live, could do such a horrible thing."

5

The map of my undoing is difficult for me to draw. I am cartographically impaired. I can navigate, sure, but I'm not linear enough to make my own charts. Was it the baby that started the depression ball heading downhill? Or was it generations of genetics and conditioning?

We were thoroughly prepared when we left the hospital. Diapers could efficiently be changed. The cord stump could effectively be swabbed. Cuddling was a go, as was general shushing and soothing. While my breasts had yet to ooze much of anything, everyone assured me that it would all work out just fine "as soon as my milk comes in." I expected my magical milk to arrive during the night like the Tooth Fairy, touching my chest with a magic wand. By the morning after this milkmaid's delivery, I would be able to feed the masses.

After only three days in the hospital, our house no longer felt like I lived there. It was clean, to start with, but the stuff in it didn't feel quite right. The cats were the most jarring. We had three at the time, which is one too many, truth be told. While pregnant, there were nights I would sob at the thought of having to get rid of them if the baby turned out to be allergic. Now, I could easily have opened the door and set them free to forage for squirrels in the garden and dodge truck-driving teenagers on the busy street. My affection for them seemed to be suffocating under thousands of layers of gauze.

It didn't help that Scott and I hadn't had any time alone with our child since her birth. At the hospital, nurses were always dashing in or out. At home, my mom would spend the day trying to take over. These first days home, she doesn't want me to do anything and wants me to stay in bed at all times, no matter what, while she takes care of everything. It's sweet, on the surface, but quickly devolves into our usual passive-aggressive routine. Subtle power shifts are at work here, with one woman trying to establish dominance over another in a covert-ops sort of way. My stepfather, bless him, stays out of it.

Physically, I don't feel that bad. I'm not saying that I could play three sets of tennis, but all things considered, I'm okay. The occasional Tylenol takes care of lingering aches. My brain and my bladder don't seem to be communicating well. If I wait too long to make a pit stop, my body will simply let the urine fall where it may. My OB waves this off as normal nerve shock after pushing for so long, but it lingers. While I'm horrified by the pee, the deflated-balloon pooch of my lower body and the continual gook I'm emitting, I'm really more tired than distraught. I know that all the physical stuff will pass. By this time next year, it will all be an amusing anecdote.

I cannot seem to settle in for a nap, however. Whenever I close my eyes, I keep flashing back on the birth. My heart starts pounding. I can't breathe. I want to flee, but have nothing tangible to flee from. My mind keeps replaying that agonizing day, trying to make it make sense. I want to call the few acquaintances I have who are mothers. "You never said it would be like that," I'd shriek, "with the fear and the pain and the helplessness." If I'd had the energy, I'd have written every last magazine editor and writer who has ever run a happy, sappy piece about the miracle of birth. I feel betrayed by all of them. There was no joy, just blood and brutality. I wonder if there's something wrong with me. Clearly, if I can't fit the trauma of birth into my head, it must be because my experience is unique—and not in a good way.

Still, it's over. The baby is out. We are all home. Good things will start now.

Eventually, we convince my mother to give us our first night alone in our own house. She leaves but reminds us that she can be back at the house in minutes if the need arises. My stepfather all but drags her out of the door.

We settle in for our inaugural voyage as new parents. The baby grows more orange by the hour and sleeps like, well, a baby, with random gurgles and grunts but without any crying. Scott and I snuggle on the couch and watch her for a bit, then try to dig through piles of e-mail and newspapers. My life starts to feel like mine again, just for a little bit.

Until we try to go to bed, which is when all hell breaks loose. The baby wakes up just as we're winding down. It would be difficult to describe what she is doing as crying. It's more like she has been possessed by devils and is screaming them out. I hike my shirt, pop off the nipple shield, and jam my boob in her mouth. She sucks, briefly, then continues to scream. I try the same thing on the other side, with the same results. I stick my pinky in her mouth, which calms her down long enough to try again with the breasts. There is no change. I am now at a loss.

I change her diaper. We rock and shush. We try again with the boobs. I am sure that there are plenty of people, my spouse included, who find my breasts worthy of further exploration. My child, unfortunately, is not one of them. The hysteria continues.

Panic has a way of feeding itself. Scott is unnerved and leaps to the conclusion that she is allergic to the cats and will soon stop breathing altogether. I am convinced that she knows that I'm not overjoyed by being a mom and is venting her wee, tearless spleen to make me look more incompetent. As he gets more frantic, the baby's volume increases and I get more frantic. After about an hour or two of this, we're both convinced that something huge is wrong, even if we disagree on the root cause. At midnight, we call the pediatrician, who essentially tells us that (a) it's too early for her to be allergic to anything, (b) that this is normal, and (c) to keep trying to get her latched on and sucking. He'll see us in the morning, since we have to come in to have the jaundice checked again anyway.

By gradual degrees, everyone calms down. Not calm enough to sleep, mind, but calm enough that the freak-out ends. The baby is held in thrall by the ceiling fan. Scott drifts off on the sofa with her in his arms. I stretch out on our bed and worry. Then the sun comes up.

The next morning, we are neither bright eyed nor bushy tailed. No one is capable of rising and shining. Instead, we lumber and fade in the bright morning light. For the first time all week, it isn't raining. Scott and I don't speak much, because the gallons of coffee have not yet kicked in. After we fumble her into her car seat, our orange baby sleeps. It's a good thing she was born in Tennessee. Her face is now the same color that Vol fans smear on their mugs during home games. That can't be good.

Even though it's a Saturday, our pediatrician is in his office. I find this stunning. I had no idea doctors would actually come in on a weekend. This is also the first time we encounter a segregated waiting room. Not "black" and "white," even though the Halls incident isn't that far in the past. One side of the waiting room is for "sick" babies; the other side for "well." This is a quandary. Technically, she is sick but she's also not contagious. To our tired minds, this is a decision of epic grandeur, even though we are the only patients there. After a good five minutes staring at both, we choose "well" but feel guilty.

The snoozing baby, the Hub, and I wait for a few minutes, then are led to a tiny room, where the baby is stripped, weighed, and poked. Through this whole ordeal, she doesn't even make a peep, not even when her pea-sized toe is pricked for a blood sample. While you don't expect newborns to perform great gymnastic feats, this listlessness isn't normal. It's like handling a hairless Oompa Loompa doll. The only thing animated are her deep blue eyes, which track our every movement, accusingly.

The nurse leaves. The baby falls back into her stupor, eyes closed. I rest my head against the edge of the exam table and count the linoleum tiles beneath my feet. Just as I start to drift to sleep, the doctor breezes in, smelling of antibacterial soap and laundry detergent. He asks a battery of questions, punctuating each answer with a nasal "Uh-huh, uh-huh." It's got a catchy rhythm, this Q&A, but I don't know if you could dance to it. The end result of this routine is that the baby's bilirubin levels are too high. It's not quite dangerous yet, but will be if remedial action isn't taken.

Jaundice in newborns is fairly common, affecting 50 to 60 percent of all infants. In most cases, jaundice corrects itself without intervention. An excess of bilirubin, which is created when red blood cells break down, causes the condition. Bruises from labor contain more degenerating red blood cells and increase the bilirubin as well. In older babies and adults, the liver can easily filter the bilirubin and pass it on to the gut, where it is disposed of in the normal course of digestive events. (Bilirubin is one of the main substances that turns poop brown.) Newborns, whose digestive systems are still immature, can have a problem dealing with the stuff.

The good news is that jaundice isn't life threatening. The bad news is that it can cause hearing loss. The even badder news is that in extreme cases, it can cause brain damage, including a type of cerebral palsy that is marked by uncontrollable tremors and/or writhing movements of the limbs. Given that jaundice doesn't reach its peak until three or four days after delivery and that the average postbirth hospital stay is down to forty-eight hours, more cases of brain damage have been reported in the last few years because extreme cases of jaundice don't develop in enough time for experienced eyes to spot them. It's still not an epidemic but it is on the rise.

According to the American Academy of Pediatrics, who know their shit about bilirubin, breastfed babies are more likely to develop jaundice, especially when they aren't nursing well. The simplest treatment for middle-grade jaundice is increasing fluids, either through breastfeeding or bottles of formula, so that the bowel and liver are flushed as frequently as possible.

The larger concern currently is that, in addition to the jaundice, the baby is becoming badly dehydrated. We're not certain if she has actually wet more than one diaper in the last twelve hours. (In our defense, modern diapers are so absorbent that it can be hard to tell if they're wet when the baby is peeing in such small amounts.) What we do know is that she is rapidly losing weight and is increasingly lethargic.

"Has your milk come in yet?" he asks.

I never knew I'd be discussing the status of my breast function with so many relative strangers. Of course, I also never thought I'd be showing my crotch to a dozen different hospital employees, so life goes on.

"Um, no," I say, and almost add, "because I am defective." I go on to explain about the breast reduction and my doula's certainty that she could get milk out of me and about how all of these people seem to have faith in my body's ability to do momlike things. And I start to go on about how important I think breastfeeding is, about how much better it is for the baby, about how much it improves IQ and overall health, about how it gives new moms a hormonal lift and helps them lose the weight, about how I've been warned by my granola friends (none of whom have kids) that pediatricians are all in the pockets of the big formula companies and will push the stuff even though we all know breast is best.

"Uh-huh, uh-huh," he says. Then he leaves the room.

He comes back with several cans of soy formula and some bottles. I want to run out of the room and put on a hair shirt. Yet another failure. This was not supposed to happen.

"Relax," he says, reading the disappointment on my face. "We have got to get some fluids into Madeline. It shouldn't interfere with breastfeeding, once your milk does come in. Keep at having her latch on and nurse. This is just temporary."

"Uh-huh," I say. "Uh-huh."

We're to come back the next day, a Sunday, simply to check her bilirubin and weight again. We will discuss options if her weight continues to fall and the bilirubin levels continue to climb. Again, I'm stunned that a doctor would be in his office on a Sunday.

We come home, emotionally wrecked. Waiting for us is my mother. Truthfully, she has never really been behind the idea of breastfeeding. I was a formula baby, as were she, her sisters, and her brother. When I'd told her my plans and launched into the spiel about the benefits of the breast, she did listen and seemed to understand my point even if she didn't agree. Still, she couldn't help but mention how much she loved her bottle when she was a tot and how much I enjoyed mine. "I didn't want to deprive you of that experience," she said. And we leave it at that.

The reality of breastfeeding is something else entirely. Deep, deep down, she is suspicious of it. All she wants to do is take the baby and a bottle and bond with her first grandchild. Instead, I am standing in the way of that, with my newfangled ideas about child rearing that spring from having liberal friends who read too many books. She must have been thrilled to see us carrying in formula, dreaming of the hours she can spend feeding this child.

I am feeling unkind at the time—exhausted, worried, spent, fearful, and isolated. My mother is not a shrew; nor is she deliberately mean. My perceptions are colored by years of us not knowing how to deal with each other. If you met her, you would love her. Really. But you are not her child. You don't have to deal with your own anger about your inability ever to make her happy. You don't have to live with the knowledge that you were the one thing that kept her from following her bliss, that you were the one who kept her in a city she hated simply because you loved your father, too. You don't have all of this baggage.

I retreat to the early-tenement bedroom with the baby and the bottles. Scott hangs back to explain the situation to my mom, who is making a big pot of soup. The baby is pretty much out of it. I put her in the portable bassinet that's been living next to our bed and give it a push to start it rocking. I open the blinds, since the pediatrician mentioned that sunlight can help break up bilirubin. I look at the formula, premixed in an easy-to-open jar. I pull up my shirt, pull out a breast, and pick up the limp child. She opens her eyes and opens her mouth. We go through the motions. I expect a miracle, flowing milk and a full child. Nothing. I start to cry.

Then I open the formula, pour some in the bottle, and stick it in her mouth. I want her to reject it, if only to offer me some small assurance that I am worthy. She sucks the formula down like a cold lemonade on a hot day, eyes wide and limbs flapping in ecstasy. An ounce is gone in no time. I burp her and put her back in the bassinet. Doesn't she know that breast is best? How can my own child reject me so soon? I cry harder, convinced that just four days in, I've already failed completely at the mom thing and that my relationship with my mom will look ideal compared to how my relationship with my daughter will turn out.

Instead of doing something sensible, like going for a brief walk to clear my head or trying to take a nap, I pick up my copy of *The Womanly Art of Breastfeeding*, the La Leche League's unofficial handbook. I found mine in a

used bookstore, but can't imagine that the information
has changed that much since 1963. After all, women have
been doing this for eons.

"After you have brought your baby into the world, the
first important step in your new role as a mother is putting your infant to your breast," the writers insist. "The
fact that you choose to take this step shows that you are
already prepared to accept the obligations—and the
joys—of motherhood. Having come this far on the road
to maturity, you will find the experience of giving yourself unstintingly to your child will bring you even further
along. In other words, one of the ways in which breastfeeding will benefit you is by helping you become a real,
more loving person, in relation to others as well as to
your child."

Finally, I have proof that I am not real, nor am I loving. This isn't a huge surprise.

Beyond this, the biggest fear I have is calling my
doula to let her know that we have failed. Scott is willing
to take the bullet, mostly because he doesn't see this as a
breastfeeding failure yet. Of course, he also hasn't spent
the last hour reading about how formula-fed babies are
more likely to be sick and stupid. Clearly, he is the more
levelheaded member of our union.

Our doula wants to talk to me, to let me know that all
hope is not lost. There is a device called a Supplemental
Nursing System, or SNS, frequently employed in situations like this. After explaining that we are far too sleepy
to be trusted to take on I-40, which is what we'd have to
do to get to the one store in Knoxville that carries these
devices, our doula offers to drive one out to our house
that evening. Again, I am stunned by the willingness of
people to give up a day off just to help us.

The day passes. Every couple of hours I give the baby more formula, which she laps up, then crashes. I can't nap when she does and use the time to stare at her or read parenting books. Every few hours, I start sobbing, provoked by absolutely nothing. But I can't stop once I start. It's like something else has taken over my body and is just wringing the tears out of it. Fortunately, the Hub gets a chance to get some real sleep, so we're not both completely useless.

Cindy shows up with a video and a bag full of stuff. The video is about how the SNS works, as well as has tips on bonding with your child. The SNS is usually employed by women who adopt children and by women with low milk supplies. As it turns out, you can breast-feed without having been pregnant, if you can adequately stimulate the breast. The body is a strange and wonderful thing.

The SNS consists of a yellow reservoir on a string, which you hang around your neck. Two tiny tubes that are about the diameter of angel-hair pasta run from it and slivers of surgical tape attach these to the breast so that the end of the tube hits the end of the nipple. The reservoir is filled with formula; the baby sucks on both tube and boob. Et voilà: a full child who is still providing the sucking needed to kick-start lactation.

Our doula sets me up the first time. After having so many people handle my breasts over the last few days, it is no longer odd. I'll pick my shirt up for practically anyone, it seems. The baby is latched on. She sucks like a vampire on the neck of a virgin. It takes forever to fill her up, because the tubes are so small and my breasts add nothing to the volume. Still, we are bonding, sort of, even though a plastic device needs to be employed in order to do so.

The doula does some math. Given the baby's weight and how much fluid she needs, we should be feeding her every two hours around the clock. Given that filling her up takes about forty-five minutes and given that the process of cleaning/hooking up the device takes another fifteen, it is going to be a long night indeed. My mom announces that she will be sleeping on the nursery floor. We're too overwhelmed to argue.

The night passes excruciatingly slowly. It takes two sets of hands to operate the SNS—one set to hold the baby in position and one to open the valve that starts the formula flowing. My mom volunteers to be the one to bring the baby to us and get the baby back to sleep. Scott takes SNS duty, filling it and cleaning it. In theory, I just have to sit there while the pit crew does the hard work and I drive the car.

It doesn't work out that way. First, my mom is one of the deepest sleepers I have ever known. She can snooze through small bombs and earthquakes. I have, on occasion, jumped repeatedly on her bed just to see if she can sleep through it. And for the record, she can. Expecting her to wake up to an alarm designed for those who aren't comatose is foolhardy. Live, learn.

Scott performed his job well, which he usually does, especially if said job involves hydraulics or levers.

I was the weakest link. Knowing, at best, that I could get only an hour of sleep at a clip left me unwilling to fall asleep at all. If I couldn't immediately drift off after the SNS circus left town, it seemed like a waste to sleep for less than an hour. After twelve hours of this, I couldn't begin even to drift off.

But the larger problem is just the wrongness of three people involved in this whole endeavor. It shouldn't take a village to feed one newborn. By the wee hours, when the feeding alarm goes off, I start to cry and continue to do so until everyone else falls asleep again.

By the next morning, we're all ragged. The baby has rediscovered that she has lungs and is screaming just because she can. She is, thankfully, less orange and a trip to the pediatrician confirms that her bilirubin levels are falling. This is good.

We keep up the two-hourly feedings. I keep up the crying. By now, I'm just sick of having so many people touching me, of never having a minute to myself to think about anything other than the baby. Rather than sleep, I search through every resource I have. Books have always provided the information I've needed to get through life. Something is just not right, but I don't know what. However, none of the words, in baby books or on the Internet, offer any solace. Everyone seems inclined to chalk up any and all wacky maternal behavior to "baby blues." I call my OB, who wants me to give it another few days, because tears and sleeplessness are fairly common during the first week.

By midafternoon, I can't function anymore. The feedings are wearing me out. Nothing is changing, breastwise. The oft-rumored milk has not come. I can't strap on the SNS again. It has become the big, yellow reservoir of my shame. So what if my kid grows up to be sick and stupid? So what if I am not giving her the best start in life I possibly can? So what if I will never be a fully loving and real person? At least, if I stop, I can get some sleep. I am selfish and weak.

"I can't do this anymore," I tell my husband, who was breastfed, because that's what his mom and his mom's mom did.

"That's . . . disappointing," he says. "But I under-stand."

He heads out to get more bottles and formula and various whatnot. I tell my mom about my decision and we scour through all of the free formula samples we've gotten in the last three months. Life moves on. For the first time in days, I nap while someone else feeds the baby. It is wonderful.

We settle into a routine, as much as you can during those first two weeks. My mom finally leaves, after much protest on her part, not ours. Scott's mom arrives. During the day, she takes charge, so much so that we're actually able to skip out and see a movie. Unfortunately, it was *Men in Black 2*. Fortunately, it didn't require all that much brain power to follow. I cry during anything too loud.

I'm glossing over a lot here, details of the esoteric sort. One day I start passing golf ball–sized blood clots. I am told to call back if they reach the size of my fist. They never do, yet my body still feels like it is possessed by some demon. I'm also glossing over the day our com-puter—our sole lifeline to the outside world, at this point—contracted some nasty virus and died. It was like losing a limb. Without e-mail, without the Web, I lose a little bit more of what keeps me tethered to my old life. It's also an amazing pain in the ass and we're forced to call a computer guy to come fix it, which he does, at con-siderable cost and by erasing everything that had been on the machine.

I'm also glossing over the good moments, those brief windows where I am in love with my Madeline, where her fingers and toes just amaze me. I am simply stunned

by the fact that my body could create something so perfect. I can't wait to see her smile for the first time. It's
hard to wait the six weeks or so until your child has the
muscular control to smile at you. Right now, it's impossible to read the expressions that float across her beautiful
face.

I take some brief naps, which make up for the fact
that I spend my nights listening to the baby in the
bassinet next to me. She can now set the whole thing
rocking herself by flailing her limbs around and the
sound of the metal runners scratching on the hardwood
floors is maddening, especially at 3 a.m.

I'm still bursting into inappropriate tears, but seem to
do okay, as long as there is a competent adult in the
house, either Scott's mom or Scott, and I can safely retreat to the bedroom when it all is too much. But no one
can stay forever. The Hub, after a brief fascination with
quitting his job, goes back to work. The next day, his
mom goes back to Rochester, New York. I wanted to
wrap myself around the legs of both of them and beg
them not to go. I don't, because I am an adult, albeit one
who is completely undone by a sub–ten-pound person
whom I don't want to be alone with.

As she leaves, Scott's mom gives me a hug and tells
me that she'll be down in a heartbeat if we need her to
be. She is serious. If I recall correctly, I believe that "job
be damned" may have been uttered. The sentiment is appreciated. I try to put on my best happy face and assure
her that we'll be just fine. I'm lying.

I don't know why I'm so terrified to be alone with my
child. We've been alone before, she and I, when she was
still floating around in my belly. Then, alone was good.

Now, my one goal is for both of us to be alive when Scott gets home. The joys of motherhood.

Despite what this litany of failings might have you believe, I am a competent adult otherwise. My job was untraditional, yes, but still involved many normal joblike things. I was in charge of a fleet of freelancers, each of whom was very fickle in his work habits and in the management style he preferred. Most of the time, I was the only woman on the editorial staff and held my own with some very opinionated men. Every week I got my stuff done—usually writing a story or two and editing the rest. We never failed to go to print because of my pages. If I may be so bold, I kicked ass in a work setting.

But the baby is something else entirely. She doesn't understand deadlines. Schedules are beyond her. Everything happens randomly. One minute she is starving; the next unconscious, or shrieking. I never know how long anything will last. She could be asleep for five hours or five minutes. There is just no way to tell. If she is awake, she wants to be rocked or held or cooed at. I can't actually do anything that is not related to these mommy duties. Most of the day, I sit on the couch and wait for whatever comes next, my hands folded in my lap, like a preschooler waiting for the next set of directions.

At this point, I give up on napping. Every time I manage to drift off, the baby wakes me up. After the tenth time, I realize that resistance is futile and just stay awake. Strangely, this isn't difficult. Sure, I'm tired, more tired than I can ever recall being, but actually falling asleep is impossible unless there is someone else in the house to tend to the inconstant child.

As a result, I start to lose my already meager ability to concentrate on pretty much everything. I can't read magazines, because I can't make sense of what the sentences mean. The TV is generally on, tuned to no station in particular, because there is nothing on during the day that can capture my interest, but I enjoy the sounds of other human voices. Every now and again, I'll pick up the baby and hold her to my chest, swaying both of us to the somber sounds of Gillian Welch's *Time (the Revelator)*. It is quite possibly the saddest album in the world, and I can't stop listening to it.

Other than that, I spend most of my "free" time either staring off into space or surfing the Internet for advice on how to get through this. Some sites are less than helpful, including one that denounces all postpartum depression as a sign that a woman is too lazy and egotistical to be a decent mother. I start to wonder if the writer is right. All of my character defects are coming home to roost. Soon I'll be the St. Francis of Fairmont Avenue, arms covered with the shitting birds of my faults. This is just the baby blues, I keep telling myself. Any day now, I'll snap out of it and understand why everyone thinks a new baby brings such joy.

By day three of my solo confinement with the baby and her thirteenth day of life, I know something is not right. I call my OB, who prescribes estrogen, which is thought to help with postpartum emotional issues, and suggests stocking up on Tylenol PM. The first night, it all works okay. I sleep, mostly, but by now am not really eating. Food holds no appeal and takes too much effort. The next night, I don't sleep, despite the drugs, and call my OB at 3 a.m. She'd been sleeping.

"The Tylenol PM isn't working. I have some Xanax. Can I take that?"

"It's not normally what we'd recommend," she tells

me, voice muzzy from hours of restful sleep. "But it'll do in a pinch. I'll call in some Ambien, a sleeping pill."

So I take the Xanax, which are left over from when I flew to the U.K. a few years previous. I still don't sleep, but no longer care that I'm awake.

By the next afternoon, I can't stop crying. I call my OB again, who prescribes Zoloft and discontinues the estrogen. The pharmacists must love me.

The problem with standard SSRIs, a class of medications which include antidepressants like Zoloft, is that they take at least two weeks to really kick in. It's not a happy pill, one that immediately lifts your mood and makes the world okay. What it does at first, frankly, is make me jumpy and nauseated. I eat a peanut butter sandwich to try to calm my stomach. It doesn't really work.

I get the itch to write down things and scrounge up an old red leather-bound travel journal that I'd gotten as a freebie from a book publisher. In it are maps, a chart of the international flag symbol codes, time zones, and dialing codes. I start on the first set of blank pages I come to, which are titled "Notes and Incidents." This, I think, qualifies as an incident.

Words are penned up inside of me. My usual outlets are gone, now that I'm not at the paper. Writing is how I've always made sense of the world, even though my prose right now is both hackneyed and clichéd. Maybe if I write this all down, it will all become illuminated. It feels important to keep a record of this, a guidebook to the inside of my head just in case I do something tragic. I want people to be able to connect the dots, later.

The Ambien doesn't work as promised. I take it after Scott gets home and sleep for two solid hours, then wake up, groggy and incoherent. For the rest of the night, I drift in and out of a light sleep, startled awake every time I can hear the skritching of the metal bassinet runners against the hardwood floor. Limbs flail up out of the rocking crib randomly, like the baby is practicing gymnastics in her sleep. By the end of the night, it's no longer cute. They start to look like tentacles from some alien species, one that mimics being human only until you turn out the lights. Then it leaps from its crib, eats your face, and sucks the life out of you. God, I'm tired.

It's about here that I'm convinced that I'm losing my mind. Increasingly, the world is becoming emotionally surreal. I start to hear music, random little snippets of songs that I haven't thought about in years. Some are commercial jingles from my childhood, some are old standards from my Bette Midler phase. The only one that sticks with me is "I just dropped in; to see what condition my condition was in," as done by Willie Nelson. I can't turn them off. I'm also getting weird visual disturbances. If I turn my head too quickly, it takes the images a couple of seconds to catch up.

I call my OB, who should be on the speed dial by now. She recommends a local shrink who specializes in postpartum depression. She also asks if I'm hearing voices. "No," I say, because it's the truth. Songs aren't really voices, are they? But I don't mention that I'm starting to think that I may be hearing voices by this time tomorrow, if I can't figure out what to do.

I call the shrink, who doesn't have an available appointment for two weeks. I take it, but don't think I can make it another twenty-four hours without some help. I start to feel vaguely let down by my medical care. My OB can't seem to help me in any meaningful way, other than to simply give me drugs. I can't see the psychiatrist when my need is the greatest. I don't know what to do, other than cry, which is the only thing I seem to be good at right now.

My doula calls, because she seems to have premonitions about these sorts of things. She sensibly tells me that I need to get someone to stay with me during the day until I am functional again. I agree, and make an appointment to meet a postpartum doula at noon the next day. My doula also suggests that I get out and take a walk, that sometimes daylight can help reset the body's clock. But it has started to rain again. Sunshine is in short supply this summer.

I call my husband, who comes home with a roll of work-related blueprints to decipher. He's (a) concerned and (b) doesn't quite know what I'll do if left alone. I don't either. I don't know where I am anymore, like the best parts of me left my body with the afterbirth. I am hollow.

From my journal, July 10:

"Two weeks old today. Hopefully, at 4:44 p.m. [the time you were born], you will still be sleeping—otherwise I will tell you happy birthday.

"Unfortunately, your mommy seems to have taken after her mommy's side of the family and sunk into a deep dark hole where she can't sleep or think or feel. I love you so much but can't express any of it. And now I'm marching under the orders of Zoloft and sleeping pills—one of the last things I wanted to have happen. While I wouldn't trade you for the world—this experience has been nothing like I expected. I suppose the option is to stop having expectations, but that wouldn't be me.

"Your father, however, is a saint.

"Today we are having thunderstorms and the power just went out. The storms are soothing, somehow, and the quasi-darkness is comforting."

I don't sleep that night, despite the ingestion of an Ambien and some Scotch left over from my thirtieth birthday. I watch the baby's limbs flail. I watch the cats watching the baby's limbs flail. The ceiling fan starts to look like a giant spider, the hairy kind with big, venom-filled fangs. My mind picks easy symbols for my inner universe. Even my breakdowns are trite. I cry. I want it all to stop, the tears, the insomnia, the failure, the feeling. I want to be empty, but there is just too much garbage ever to feel new and clean. I am worthless.

The night passes, but just barely.

Scott, after he wakes up, takes one look at me and suggests we call his mother to see if she'll come back down. He looks shaken, not like himself. Later, when pressed, he describes my appearance as "vacant."

He absolutely has to go to work that morning, but leaves a message for his mom, who is currently at work. I promise him that I can make it until he can come home in the afternoon. I also promise that I will call my OB again and be brutally honest with her.

Before he leaves, I jump in the shower. I suddenly remember my mom's old razor that always rested in the shower of whatever apartment we lived in. It was the old-school type, a black plastic handle with a shiny metal head. You unscrewed the bottom to put new blades in. As a toddler, I was fascinated by it, so much so that I once picked it up by the sharp end, slicing the palm of my hand in a couple of places. Even more magnetic were the small white rectangles of paper-wrapped razor blades. They were in a spring-loaded container and you could pop them out and push them back in without hurting yourself. Unless, of course, the paper tore. Then you could do some damage.

All that I have in my shower are cheap disposables. They are just barely sharp enough to remove leg stubble, much less break the skin. But there are knives in the kitchen.

I can see the blood running down my hands, like stigmata. It mixes with the shower water and drips, pinkly, off of my fingertips. I am so tired. Now I can rest.

But I can't, not really. My wrists are whole. There is no blood. Just me, in the shower, with some Dial soap and a bath poof.

"You okay?" Scott asks, with that furrow he gets between his eyebrows when he's thinking very hard. "You were in there a while."

"I'm fine," I lie. "But I don't know what to do next."

We call my OB and get her answering service. After I again promise that I will keep it together until he gets back, Scott leaves for work. I wait, hands clenched in my lap, and hope someone calls me back soon.

6

Crazy mothers are nothing new.

The earliest may be Margery Kempe, born in 1373 (or so). Kempe has long been ballyhooed in academic circles as the first woman to write an autobiography. Since she was illiterate, as most woman and poor men were at the time, she is technically the first woman ever to dictate an autobiography.

Kempe, the daughter of a burgess, was hailed by some as a Christian mystic/martyr who was visited by the Almighty in order to educate others about the true nature of evil. For me, at least, it's most telling that Kempe's first round of visions hit her just after the birth of her first child. At the time, she owned a brewery but her beer went flat because she disappointed the Lord. After her childbed madness and busted business, Kempe took to the road as a preacher, spreading the word to others that true joy would be found only after death.

Her wanderings were met with hostility. Frequently, Kempe was told to "give up this life you lead, and go and spin, and card wool, as other women do" (as quoted in Roy Porter's book *Madness*). She did, in a sense, devote herself to fiber crafts and took to wearing a hair shirt while additionally shunning all sexual contact with her spouse. Eventually, they received the medieval equivalent of a divorce. He agreed to give up any rights to her body in exchange for her paying off all of his debts, which, if nothing else, proves that patterns of human behavior tend not to change.

Kempe began to have more visions and, according to Porter, "these were accompanied by the copious bouts of weeping which attended her to the end of her days. . . . Her weeping bouts were detested, she was called a 'false hypocrite' and her friends were advised to abandon her. Furthermore, she was accused of having the Devil in her and of being a 'false Lollard,' that is, heretic. But such trials enhanced her awareness of the divine indwelling. When she heard mention of Christ's Passion, she would swoon in ecstasy and experience divine music."

Eventually, Kempe made a pilgrimage to the Holy Land, where she came unglued completely. Some observers believed her to be an epileptic. Others thought her possessed by evil spirits. Her fellow English travelers thought she was faking it simply to be a nuisance. Kempe was booted from their party and ran the risk of being chucked in jail for behavior unbecoming to a wife and mother. After this trial, she "married" God in a vision and announced her chastity to all but Him. She still wrote of the fleshy temptations sent to her by the Devil, but her confessors helped keep her on the righteous path.

So did God actually speak to Kempe or was she simply insane? From the scant evidence we have, I can step onto a shaky limb and say that sounds like classic postpartum psychosis. All of her mania can be dated to the birth of her first child, she was hearing voices, and frequently suffered from crying spells. But my immediate response to people who believe that God is talking to them directly is to leap to the conclusion that they're completely nuts. The line between madness and religious experience has always been vague, but I am probably not the most impartial judge on this matter. If you ask me, a priest, and a women's studies PhD, you'll get three wildly different answers.

Regardless of whether or not Kempe was truly one enchilada short of a combo plate or simply God-touched, she wasn't the first woman to lose her mind after having a baby. But these women are hard to dig up. First, history has a tendency to ignore women in general unless they do something spectacular or globally noteworthy. While I can find a couple of dozen diaries from average men in any given century, the average woman, apart from the odd midwife or nun, kept fairly quiet, partly because she was illiterate. Their lives were in the private sphere, confined mostly to child and hearth behind closed doors. Plus, it's hard to track someone who loses her name when she gets married and simply becomes Mrs. John Doe.

Second, and perhaps most important, madness tends to be shoved under the rug because it is so stigmatized. No one has known what to do about the insane for most of modern history. Various remedies have been imposed—from turning them loose in the countryside to eugenics to radical surgeries to asylums to chemicals and electronics—but none has ever really proven to be all that effective. And most right-thinking people were disinclined to study the mentally ill, because the condition has long been believed to be the patient's fault, either because she didn't live a fine, upstanding life or because she was being punished by God. The question of what to do with the insane is still a very real concern, one with no clear answers.

Third, and perhaps the aspect we talk about the least, is that most crazy people are scary to the outside observer, objects of fear and derision rather than compassion. The mentally ill are unpredictable and capable of inhuman acts. That's part of the definition. If you have a mental illness, you have lost some control of your thought processes, emotions, or moods. As Hinkley or Dahmer or Booth proved, crazy people are capable of violence, sometimes on a massive scale. And it's worse somehow if you're a mother, that paragon of nurturing virtue who could never harm a hair on the head of a child, much less drown one in the tub to drive out the devils that only she sees. Here's the one person in society who is looked on as pure and loving and she turns out to be just as human as everyone else, subject to the same perversions we all are. It's subversive and un-American. Next we'll find out that baseball players cheat and that apple pie is actually French. Mothers who go mad are a terrifying paradigm shift, on the order of priests who fondle young boys. Sweeping it all under the rug is less terrifying than looking the reality in the face, because this face seriously messes with our worldview.

"I reluctantly enclose application filled out for admission of my mother," wrote a respected bank employee to the superintendent of the Wisconsin Hospital for the Insane in 1875. "Of late she has grown materially worse, so that we deem it unsafe for the female portion of the family to be left alone with her during the day and especially for the little 2 year old that is obliged to remain continually there, as she has stated several times of late that she or the children must be sacrificed. Should she destroy another us [*sic*] could never forgive ourselves if the state has a place provided for their comfort and possible need" (from Gerald N. Grob's *Mental Illness and American Society*, 1875–1940).

The women who made it to an asylum were the lucky ones. Most were left to their own devices with disastrous results. A Philadelphia woman, Marie Noe, was believed to be the most unlucky mother alive, a title bestowed on her by *Life* magazine in 1963. Starting in 1949, Noe had ten kids, each of whom died. Their deaths were chalked up to SIDS, a condition that we still don't know all that much about. But we do know that an adult can suffocate a child with relative ease and without detection. All of her babies died when Noe was the only one in the house with them. At the time, no one raised an eyebrow, but years later, the case ignited the investigatory fires of Jamie Talan and Richard Firstman, whose 1997 book *The Death of Innocents: A True Story of Murder, Medicine, and High-Stake Science* caused the Noe case to be reopened. In 1999, Noe confessed to killing eight of her ten kids. The now 70-year old Noe struck a plea bargain and was sentenced to twenty years' probation. With this case and with so many like it, we may never know whether the mother is profoundly cursed by the baby gods or smothered her own kids in a postpartum haze. But it does make one wonder what the real statistics may be.

Not all mothers who lose their minds will kill their kids. Most won't, in fact. About 80 percent of new mothers suffer from what is called the baby blues, mild periods of weeping and emotional instability that clears up during the first two postpartum weeks. It isn't fun, of course, but it isn't debilitating. Next on the scale is postpartum depression, which gets worse after the first two weeks and affects up to 20 percent of new mothers, one in every five. It is characterized by the classic clinical depression symptoms like insomnia, diminished interest in almost every activity, anxiety, excessive guilt, panic attacks, and suicidal thoughts.

With each passing year, these depressed mothers are also more likely to get the kind of help that they need, because postpartum depression has become more recognized. It's still shameful, of course, but thanks to high-profile confessions from luminaries such as Brooke Shields and Marie Osmond, the condition is reluctantly being accepted as a real medical emergency rather than a character flaw.

But the most debilitating form of postpartum mental illness is postpartum psychosis. It grabs all the headlines because it is unusual and, if left untreated, gruesome. Andrea Yates, the Houston mom who drowned her kids, is the classic example of psychosis. Less than 1 percent will develop this illness, but its symptoms are hard to deny. It is marked by hallucinations, delusions (frequently, these involve religious imagery), and disordered thought. This manifestation of mental illness is a medical emergency. It won't vanish on its own. It is not the result of a weak character or moral flaw. It can't just be walked off. Psychosis is as serious as a stroke and, finally, decent treatments exist for it that do work.

Sadly, no such treatments existed in West Virginia during the early 1900s. Crazy mothers had no place to go and would frequently vanish when the psychological burdens became too overwhelming. One such woman was my great-grandmother Elizabeth Flowers Hendershot Cain, who abandoned her three kids—one of whom was Nell, my grandmother—under mysterious circumstances. We've never known much about Elizabeth. We know that she had Nell, the middle child, in 1912, which would have made Elizabeth sixteen years old then. The first child, Ruth, must have been born when Elizabeth was thirteen or fourteen, which boggles my mind. At thirteen, I was still playing with Barbies.

The only picture that anyone can find of Elizabeth shows a big-eyed woman in an even bigger flowered hat. A tall blond man wearing a suit, a striped dress shirt, and a tie stands behind her. There are two little girls—maybe ages five and eight—in the foreground. They have on white dresses, white tights, white hair bows, and black boots. One of the little girls looks like Nell, and by extension, then, also looks like my mother, my daughter, and me. Judging by the clothes, I'd pin the year somewhere in the late 1910s or early 1920s, which would be about right. Elizabeth would have been in her mid-twenties, then.

But here's the real kick in the head. I can't promise you that any of this is true. The picture is undated and unlabeled. My mother found it in a box with nine dozen other snapshots, which were discovered after my grandfather died a few years ago. The people in this picture could be almost anyone, despite the fact that one of them looks like a relation. And, importantly, the youngest kid, a boy, is missing. He may simply have not been alive when the photo was snapped, in which case my dates are probably off. Or it may be that this photo is of someone my granddad knew at the dairy or in Colorado or is something he bought at a thrift store for a nickel because he liked the lady's hat. It's all a big mystery.

While every life has meaning to someone, Elizabeth wasn't the kind of woman who made much of a mark on the larger world. Given that no one in my immediate family even thought about this great-grandmother until a decade ago, after my cousin Julie had her first child and her first bipolar episode, we have made remarkable progress discovering information about her. The little information we have scraped together at this late date is all we're ever going to get.

No one even knows where Elizabeth is buried, or what she did before she died, or where she spent most of her life. My mom and the sisters knew only that she had died in 1955 or '56, and that information was only gleaned by remembering how distraught Nell had been when she received a letter from home that mentioned that her mother had died. No one ever talked about Elizabeth before then or, truth be told, much after that. She never really existed in their minds until they were much older and found the silences suspicious.

Nonetheless, dry facts about Elizabeth's death were easy to find, once I found the right person to ask. She died on January 9, 1956, and had just celebrated her fifty-ninth birthday. She died in a house on Third Street, which was near the flood wall in downtown Parkersburg. Today, it's the site of a car dealership, but, then, it was probably the seediest area this tiny town had. Her official place of residence was with her sister, Carrie Smart, of Columbia Avenue. Elizabeth's occupation was housewife, but her state of "conjugal relations" was divorced. The principal cause of death was listed as "chronic alcoholism," which very well may have been the case. Family rumors allege that she drank to combat the depressions that routinely beset her. Given how many of her descendants wrestle those demons, it's an easy rumor to believe. But not an easy one to prove.

If you can find a date of death, you can usually find an obituary, especially in a small-town paper. Only I couldn't. For the first hour of searching in the local library, I wondered if I'd screwed up a date somewhere and had the wrong reel of microfilm. This is exactly the sort of dunderheaded mistake that I make on a routine basis. While the fault was indeed mine, it was that I'd assumed her obit would be with the rest of the obits, buried on an interior page. Instead it was front-page news.

In the January 10, 1956, edition of the *Parkersburg News*, next to headlines like "Death Penalty Demanded for Dope Peddlers" and "Roads Glazed, Travel Risky, Area Shivers," is an innocuous story titled "Death Here Investigated." It reads:

Coroner Richard Corbitt was called to 130½ 3d St., around 7 o'clock last night after City Police had been notified that Mrs. Elizabeth Flowers Cain, 59, had been found dead.

Dr. Corbitt after examination said the woman came to her death from natural causes.

She was removed to the Franklin funeral home.

She had been making her home with her sister, Mrs. Carrie Smart at 648 Columbia Av., and then left there and went to a friend's home on Mary St., and then left there and went to the 3d St. address.

She told a friend there she was cold and was told to go get in bed and cover up, according to the police investigating. This was around 3:30 p.m. When found four hours later she was dead.

She is survived by two daughters: Mrs. W. M. Reese of Takoma Park, Md., and Mrs. W. C. Tebay of Grand

Junction, Colo.; one son, Arthur Cain, Jr., of Parkersburg; the sister with shom [*sic*] she resided, seven grandchildren and several cousins.

Services . . .

My mother actually started crying when I gave her this rundown of what I'd been able to find. Her response illustrates how very little we know about her family's past. Just this small packet of facts equates to five times more than anyone previously knew. It makes the phantom Elizabeth real. And the thought of that real woman dying alone and cold and alienated haunts me. That's what happens to a stray dog, and even that would make me raise an eyebrow. I can't ever know what really happened, but, no matter how difficult my own relationship with my mom has been, I can't ever imagine letting her die like that. And, knowing my great-grandmother's fate, I can't help but dislike Nell and her siblings, just a little bit.

To them, Elizabeth was an unperson. In Nell's engagement announcement, which merited a lengthy article in the pages of the local daily, she is described as the daughter of Mr. Arthur R. Cain of Wheeling and the niece of Mrs. James D. Cooper, the married name of the aunt who raised them. Nowhere is her mother even mentioned. My mom and the aunts were shocked to discover that the woman they knew as Aunt Carrie—the one who came over to clean the house when Nell was at her worst—was actually their real aunt, Elizabeth's sister Carrie Smart. There are so many questions that could have been answered then, had they known and been old enough to care. It's so hard for kids to winkle these sorts of things out of parents who are determined not to acknowledge them.

It angers me, frankly, this denial of a woman's life.

Times were different, I know, and I'm approaching this from a twenty-first-century perspective where better living through chemistry is possible. I know the temptations of denial, of wanting to push away everything that hurt you in the past in order to preserve yourself. The shame that must have washed over Nell when she discovered that her crazy mother's death had made front-page news must have been debilitating. Still, I'm pissed that I never got the chance to know any of this, to have this decision made for me because someone else was scared. But, as my aunt said, shit is something you flush away.

Sadly, this particular poo floats.

Both in age and personality, my cousin Julie and I are probably the closest of all of my relatives. We're nine months apart and, as the years have passed and pounds have been gained and lost by both parties, we look amazingly similar. At family gatherings, we'd always sneak off to create a "show," which featured singing and comedy skits, talents that we'd honed from a shared love of *Saturday Night Live*. Our moms have the videotapes of these works of genius stashed in a box, ready to be unleashed on the unsuspecting at a moment's notice.

There are differences between us, of course. I always had my head in a book while Julie was more outgoing, a former Miss Teen of Florida who placed in the top ten in the national competition. Our Aunt Donna, one of our grandfather's many siblings, always labeled me the "smart" one and Julie the "pretty" one, which was unfair on a number of levels, but is convenient shorthand.

We'd probably be even closer if we'd grown up in the same place. Distance—with me in Pittsburgh and her outside of Orlando—got in the way. Then as we got older, our paths were different. I fell into college and dropped out of the family's sight intentionally; Julie struggled with school but found her future family with a boy named Drew, who she married in her early twenties, shortly before giving birth to her first child. I have a picture of her at my wedding, which was three months after hers. She and a cousin are standing back-to-back, both with undeniable pregnant bellies and huge grins. There's no way to warn her of what's to come.

After the baby's birth, Julie dropped out of sight. My mom would pass on scattered reports about psych wards but did not convey the severity of Julie's situation. This was partly my fault. I was so focused on getting my own personal postcollege act together that I couldn't quite care about anyone else's problems. I want to blame this solely on the myopia of being in my early twenties, but, actually, I've always been like this. I do think it is all about me.

But Julie and her mother Linda were also good at playing the crazy cards close to their chests. The sheer fact that Julie was mentally ill came as a total shock to everyone. In hindsight, it should have been amazingly clear that this could happen. But Julie's psychiatric adventure is what finally made everyone wake up to the family's past and own it for what it is and what it has reaped. We weren't there yet when Julie took ill—and we were ill equipped to talk about it at the time.

Now, however, we have the words. Rather than impose my own interpretation on the events, mostly because I wasn't there, I will let Julie tell it herself. For the record, Julie and Drew and Hannah aren't their real names. Currently, Julie is living in a small town in the South where she feels the perceptions of any mental illness, particularly a mother's, are negative and closed-minded.

Julie's story goes like this:

"My immediate family really protected me. They tried to guard me and let me tell my story and let me have some privacy for my sake. They tried to let me tell what I was comfortable telling. That's why I think a lot of people—friends or family or anyone—didn't know as much. My mom and Drew didn't know if I wanted people to know or if I wanted it to be a secret. At the time, you don't know if you want people to know.

"In hindsight, I had problems before but I didn't really figure it out. Let's see—Hannah was born on Monday morning, that would be Day One. Day Two, I left the hospital around noonish. They were trying to push me out the door. I hated it. You just watch this baby care video and you have to go through your discharge, you have to do this, you have to do that—you have to do all of these things to check out. I was like—I can't get out as fast as you want me to. I took my time and still they got me out the door by 2 p.m.

"I have in my mind that my mother went home on Thursday. I remember holding Hannah and maybe vacuuming. I remember holding her in the kitchen and I felt like she had a fever and it scared me. Her head always feels hot—babies have a hot head. I had an anxiety attack—but I did not know what an anxiety attack was. To me, an anxiety attack can be like being scared of a bear but there's no bear in the room. I started calling them episodes because I didn't know what they were.

"Because of my faith, I always think of Scripture and how God doesn't want us to fear. I'd say to myself 'I shouldn't fear' but I was. I couldn't help it. Really, I've definitely seen through the course of time that my relationship with God and my faith have definitely been a plus. I've prayed my heart out and I've seen what I believe to be God's blessings. It is one of the strengths that holds me together. But you cannot pray yourself out of a manic episode or an anxiety attack. You can't.

"A lot of times when I get sick I say, 'Is this who I am? Is this my character? Is this me? How can I be this way?' You do things that are embarrassing or stupid or dumb. Things that you're not proud of. But I have over time realized that it is your chemicals, like cancer or diabetes or a cold. It's not something you can control. You've got to have medication. You've got to.

"I remember going to the pediatrician at the one-week checkup—that would have been Monday of the following week. I remember lying on the couch in the pediatrician's office and drinking my water bottle, because I was having an episode and I was describing that to her. I remember what I was wearing and lying down on the couch in the office.

"Also, I was breastfeeding, so I was up all the time. There was one morning, shortly after my mom left, I was in the bathroom at night and I remember feeling like I was going crazy. I don't know if I was having diarrhea, because that goes along with my anxiety attacks. It's disgusting but that's part of anxiety attacks, that and feeling like I'm going to throw up, but not throwing up.

"But I felt like I was going crazy. I thought of Uncle Bill. And I thought—I am going crazy. I can't explain it, but I remember at the time I felt like I was going crazy and I wanted to call my mother. Drew did not want me to call. 'It's three in the morning,' he said. 'You can't call your mom and wake her up. Now, *that's* crazy.'

"I did eventually call her. She told me to have a bowl of cereal and read something positive. I remember sitting at the table and having a bowl of Raisin Bran and reading an article in *Guideposts*. Maybe that helped me calm down. And, of course, Hannah didn't have a fever.

"Ever since that one time, throughout the last ten years, if my kids have a fever or if they start getting sick, I feel sick. It just kicks off anxiety immediately. I think I've gotten better over the years but, still, it's an automatic response. I'm like—I know she'll be fine, but my body goes into an anxiety attack. I know that, logically, everything's okay.

"I knew I was going crazy that third or fourth night at home."

Drew interjects. "You did not. You were barely coherent."

"I was going a mile a minute," Julie says. "I was in my own world. What else would you say about me?"

"You didn't really know where we were going," Drew says.

"I remember being in the doctor's office. Didn't I go behind his desk?"

"You didn't realize why we were there," Drew says.

"I remember the bag, the red canvas striped bag that I took with me with all of the pictures I had been taking. That was something that I had been doing with all of my busybody stuff and making a mess. In the car, I was constantly writing in my little notebooks, like I do whenever I get manic. I write passionately. I have to write everything down, even if it's gibberish and random unconnected thoughts. They might make sense to me."

"It's English," Drew adds. "The words do make sense."

"What prompted us to go to the doctor?"

"Because my wife was crazy. It was obvious. Even somebody like me, who has never run into someone crazy before, knew that I had to take you to the doctor."

"I do remember that I was a busybody, all over the house. I think I thought I was getting things done, but I wasn't. I was just making a huge mess. And I was taping things to the wall. I had papers all over the floor, papers I was sorting out like how to take care of babies. They were at the foot of the bed and I must have had twenty stacks. I was sorting. I remember tacking stuff up on the wall, like instructions by the sink on washing hands and taking care of your breasts. And I wanted to put on a production and film it out in the front yard, like a *Saturday Night Live* skit. There was something about making someone dress in a trenchcoat. I was just busy, busy with pictures. I was posing Hannah with pictures and putting all of the flowers behind her. And I actually got a really cute picture. Doing pictures always goes along with my mania.

"So we went to my doctor. I want to say what he gave me was Nembutal. It should knock you out. It did not knock me out. I thought I slept, but Drew said I did not sleep. We're back in his office the next day. Hannah was ten days old. He suggested that we go to the closest mental hospital. So we go over there and they're interviewing me. And I remember telling them about Grandma Nell, and what everyone suspected about her. And that I had an uncle who went crazy and committed suicide. I was afraid—I didn't have a suicidal thought, but I was afraid that I would feel that way, afraid that I would do what he did. I remember trying to lie on the floor and drink water. The admitting nurse is asking me things like 'People with glass houses . . .' and I was supposed to finish it with '. . . should not throw stones.' Instead I said '. . . should not go around naked.' It's true!

"I was there eight days. They put me on Depakote and Risperdal. And the Risperdal would make my tongue lock up, like stiffen. So they gave me some beta-blocker so that side effect wouldn't happen. I had really dry mouth, and I didn't know what all was going on.

"They sent me to group therapy, which was a joke. They had people in there who had been sodomized, a woman whose father had incest with her, and people who were alcoholics. I had to hear all of that kind of therapy being discussed and be a part of that. I'm like, 'No. I am a new mother. I just had a baby. This is not where I belong. This is not the way it should be.' I asked the medical director. He said that they had maybe one case every three years. They rarely have a postpartum psychosis so they don't know how to deal with it. I didn't have Hannah—somebody else had to take care of Hannah. She could visit, but because I was taking the Depakote and whatever, I couldn't breast-feed her. So I was pumping my breasts and throwing it out. A couple of the techs, I was showing them how to use the breast pump. I remember them just sitting there, because they had to sit with me if I used the breast pump, because it had a cord.

"The first night I was there—I didn't know that you could go get your own towels. I didn't know about that. The shower was level with the whole tile floor. There was no protection from the shower and the rest of the bathroom. The floor is all even. So I take a shower and there's water all over the floor. I got my socks wet—and I only had the pair of socks that I had on. I remember complaining that 'Y'all need to come clean this up.' I called down to housekeeping, calling down there and calling down there. Then I get agitated and angry because I'm in my state. One of the techs, I said something to him, then he tells me that I can get towels and I can take care of it. Then he says 'Well, you shouldn't turn the water on so hard, so then it won't spray all over.' To this day, I don't think I can turn on a water faucet without thinking about how mad that made me, that they wouldn't come help me and that I had to figure it out for myself.

"All I had were the towels and I couldn't dry my hair, so I went to bed with wet hair. Later, I got to use a hair dryer, but I had to use it in front of them. And I can remember wanting to go outside—they had this little outer area that was closed in—but I remember not being able to go outside. And not being able to get out the door. It was like being in jail.

"As for the family, I think it's obvious that there's a genetic predisposition to the illness, like if your uncle had heart disease or your sister had breast cancer. We have the gene, whatever the genes are, we have them. I don't blame that on our family. I think part of it is genetics and part of it is environment and stress. We read, when this happened, that a lot of times bipolar disorder comes out around our age for women, around the twenties and a lot of times after childbirth or some very stressful experience. The childbirth was the thing that kicked it off for us. Your chemicals are going nuts, it's high stress and sleep deprivation. And the stress of the pain just overwhelmed everything. I think that with everything that goes along with having a baby, if you have the genetics for it, then it just comes out.

"I know granddad was a drinker, but I don't know that he was mentally ill. I always thought granddad was pretty stable. He was well educated and successful, but Nell, I think, was scattered. Mom remembers—especially since she's been coming to see me—Mom remembers they always had help. She remembers the house being a mess, memories of her childhood like that. That's what makes it harder for her to come into my home—it's like a tornado hit it and my mother's a neat freak. She said to me—how are you going to teach the kids to pick up after themselves if you don't pick up after yourself? And then I wanted to say—you set the example for me and it doesn't seem to have worked.

"One of the lessons to learn from this, which is key, is that since you and I have children, when they get ready to have babies, we need to be there for them. It may or may not come out in our children."

Seven years after Hannah's monumental arrival, Julie discovered she was pregnant again.

"To me," she says, "this is an incredible story. We had a couples' group Bible study, which ended up in a large group. This was in August—I wish I had the date and I wish I had the church bulletin (and, knowing me, I did save it). The day's sermon was 'I'll tell you whom to fear, fear the Lord.' Which really means having reverence for the Lord but not fearing other things, not living in fear. Trusting in God.

"So the question, when we broke up into small groups, was 'What do you fear that you're not trusting God with?' And I said, we would like to have other children, but I don't want to have to be on medication because I'm afraid of what it will do to the baby. I'm afraid of having the postpartum psychosis again. Everyone had their own thing that was shared and was prayed for, but we couldn't make the decision. We found out on October 23 that I was pregnant. The conception day was September 26. I was on the Pill, hadn't taken antibiotics or anything. It would have been one cycle after that church meeting. I feel like God made that decision for me. He said, okay, it's time. And you can trust me.

"As soon as I found out, I drank a ton of Gatorade and stopped taking the lithium immediately. That's what you do to try to flush it through. I'd never called my doctor at home except when I found out I was pregnant. I called and left a message on his answering machine— 'I'm pregnant!'

"After baby number two was born, I had specific instructions on what to do. It was mainly to take my medicine to help me think clearly and to get some sleep. I had a lot of support where someone else took the baby during the night and I didn't wake up. From the start she was on formula. Everything stayed even and fine because I had my doctor and I had the medication. I had no problems with her.

"I still have manic episodes but not as bad. There have been different bumps in the road. In 2002, in May, I decided I wanted to lose weight. I had gained weight because of one of my medications. I started out when I got married at a hundred and seventeen pounds, then I gained at least thirty pounds. I lost twenty pounds right off the bat, but I've stayed twenty pounds heavier than where I started.

"I hated my first doctor. He was someone who'd just been assigned to me out of the blue. I didn't get to choose a nice psychiatrist before I had the baby. I picked an OB. Who knew? On December 9, I just quit taking my medicine altogether.

"You know what was really funny? In the first psych hospital, they had a deck of cards. Some of the cards were missing, so people had written 'Ace of Spades' or 'Ten of Clubs' on other cards to make it a full deck. There was this one guy who was real edgy and agitated, and I was giving him the cards to play with. I was explaining to him that this is not a full deck. And he said to me: 'Don't tell me I'm not playing with a full deck.' This crazy guy said this to me!"

Then she laughs and sounds just like the cousin I have always known.

7

After I admit that I have to get some help and get as far as the gas station, where I fill up my car and am ignored by strangers, I can't even pretend to keep my meager wits together anymore. By the time I make it to the ER, I'm crying so hard I can't speak. An Aunt Bea–like woman seated behind the desk peers over at me, takes in my tie-dyed T-shirt, ill-fitting maternity shorts, and sneakers, as well as the fact that I'm dripping rain water all over the spotlessly clean floor, and doesn't even raise an eyebrow. This hospital—the same one where I gave birth to the baby—is in what Realtors would call a "transitional" area. On any given weekend night, crime-related gunshot victims mix with drunken frat boys from the university and neurotic upper-middle-class Victorian house restorers from the nearby gentrified neighborhood. Here, a public housing project is a five-minute drive from some of the higher priced houses in Knoxville, the city that zoning forgot. Given the odd social mix, the grocery store just down the hill from the hospital is called the Fellini Kroger. There, a good friend once spotted a man wearing an apron covered in blood who was pushing a cart full of half-gallons of vanilla ice cream through the store on an otherwise dull weekday evening. It's that kind of place.

During Aunt Bea's appraisal, I fumble out my driver's license and insurance card and fling them at her. She taps at her computer. "You had a little girl two weeks ago?" I nod. I don't sit down. I don't want to get the chair all wet. "What brings you here?" I give her a brief sketch between sobs, starting with the not sleeping and ending with the phone conversation I'd just had with my OB's nurse practitioner, during which she told me to leave the baby with someone safe and get my rear to the ER with all reasonable haste. I almost empty the box of tissues on the counter next to Aunt Bea's machine.

"Go sit over there," she says, not unkindly, gesturing to the waiting room. The only other folk experiencing emergencies on this particular weekday afternoon are an elderly couple, the female half of whom has an unstoppable bloody nose, and a gentleman with a mullet and a NASCAR shirt whose injuries remain unknown to me. Snippets of songs are rattling around in my head, which they've been doing for the last couple days. It is nothing like those little earwigs we all get, the tunes that haunt your quasiconscious mind for a day or two before vanishing. This is a relentless mix of one or two lines from a half-dozen songs. It was like living with a car radio that randomly skipped stations for hours on end. I can't turn it off. If nothing else sends you around the bend, this will. I still wonder if this was a side effect of simple sleep deprivation or a sign that I was about to crack up completely.

I cry while I wait, naturally, and wonder what the parking lot attendant must have thought of me as I handed him a damp wad of singles. Did he think I was visiting a dying relative? Or did he know that I had officially lost my shit and was about to check myself into the nuthatch? Were weeping women just part of his routine workday? Or was I special, somehow, young and puffy and a break from the monotony of older folks visiting even older folks or doctors rushing to the office? I'm sad that I don't know. He did smile, however, which was nice.

Eventually I'm shuttled into a little room, where my blood pressure and temperature are taken. Unlike most women in Knoxville, the nurse is brusque and abrasive, like it's her job to make sure I'm not trying to pull one over on my insurance company or just faking a nervous breakdown in order to spend a week in bed eating hospital food. Which probably is her job, come to think of it.

At her request I have to run through the last two weeks again. Over the next five days, I will tell this story so many times that I consider setting it to music and having it recorded, so that telling it is more interesting for me. If I were Arlo Guthrie, I would add some four-part harmony and a nifty chorus à la "Alice's Restaurant."

"My OB's office sent me here," I tell her. "I just talked to her."

"Why?"

"I told her someone else should raise the baby"— despite the number of times I'll say this, I never once manage to get through that phrase without coming completely unglued, which I do now; rivers of snot threaten to run onto my shirt—"because I just can't do it."

"Where will you be?"

"I don't know. Gone." And with that word, a plastic bracelet is slapped on my wrist. Should I lose my mind enough to forget my name, it is helpfully attached to the end of my left arm. I sign enough forms to make paper-company executives dance with unbridled joy at the profits. The humorless nurse makes me sit in a wheelchair, which is handed off to a younger, equally humorless nurse. I wonder how they get through their dreary days. Maybe there's a mariachi band sequestered in a storage closet or the staff dips into the narcotics during coffee breaks.

I am led to an exam room in an out-of-the-way corner of the ER. A guard is posted by my door, which is to remain open at all times. He is armed and all of twenty. If I get up to pee, he waits outside the bathroom. I wonder what he'd do if I tried to off myself in my room. Burst in and shoot me, maybe. The guard tries conversational gambits like "Feeling a little sad, huh?" and "It happens, you know." Every now and again, he'll stick his head into the exam room and ask, "You okay?" I don't know how to answer any of this. I don't know what the etiquette is in these sorts of situations.

Spalding Gray's doppelgänger is the first doctor I see, which echoes tragically in my memory after Gray's own suicide. I hope for a witty, pathos-rich monologue that can give me some Down East perspective on what is going on. I get only deadpan, affectless questions. He and the nurses must have gone to deadpan school together. They certainly have emptied enough deadpans on me. I tell the story again—no harmonies, no catchy chorus. He asks if I'm on any drugs, legal or illegal. He asks if I've thought about hurting myself. I start to tell him about my shower that morning, but don't. The shame makes me choke it back. He tells me about the Tower 4 day program, where I could sleep at home and come to the unit just for group therapy. The last place I want to be is at home, where the baby is and where I'll have to be alone with her. "The nights are the hardest part," I choke and proceed to sob too hard to continue. "Spalding" makes a couple of notes, orders a few blood tests, then leaves.

Another person—male, but tiny this time—comes in to draw blood. He's trollish, which I don't mean unkindly. He just looks like he should live under a bridge and not let any billy goats cross it. He's a nice guy, who tells me all about his wife and his passel of kids. He keeps up a steady stream of words while tapping my deep, tiny veins, which have driven other lab techs to drink. He pats me on the arm when he's done. "You'll be okay," he tells me. I want to believe him.

Two hours have elapsed since I'd talked to my OB's office. After I hung up with them, I called Scott, who told me to bring the baby to his place of employ, The Bijou, a restored downtown-movie-house-now-live-theater where he worked as the technical director. The office staff, which also includes a nurse from this same hospital who also moonlights at the theater, could easily take care of the baby. He offered to come home to drive us both where we needed to be. I declined, because my OB's nurse practitioner had made it clear that I was to take the baby to him, then come to the hospital. Once I'd been given a plan, I couldn't dream of deviating from it. (In hindsight, of course, there was no reason to do it that way—but I have always been very good at following instructions.) After I hung up with him, I called the postpartum doula, Kimberly, to whom my birthing doula had introduced me and with whom I had an appointment later that afternoon. The message I left didn't make a lot of sense, but I did mention that I was on my way to the ER.

My set of operating instructions for the next few hours wrapped me in a blanket of toasty calmness. The crying and the song snippets stopped for a bit while I gathered the baby and chucked supplies into the diaper bag. I remembered to pack formula and an ice pack into

an insulated lunchbag. I replenished the supply of diapers and wipes. I added a blanket, a change of clothes,
and her toy lion, which she seemed to like, as much as
you can tell with a two week old who can't smile yet.

I strapped her into the car seat, grabbed my wallet,
then walked out to the car, where I loaded the car seat.
This was our first official solo car trip together. It felt like
we should mark this occasion somehow, with balloons
and champagne maybe, but these were not forthcoming.
The thought passed as quickly as it came.

We drove. The baby didn't make a peep the whole
way; I cried softly. I'd like to say that there was something remarkable about that ten-minute trip. There really
wasn't.

I got to the theater. Scott met me by the loading dock
and took the baby, car seat, and diaper bag. He told me
to wait a minute, that he would run her upstairs, where
many hands could make light work of babysitting, and
go to the ER with me. I said no. That wasn't what I'd
been told to do. He asked if I'd be okay by myself. I said
yes, that I wanted the baby to be with her daddy, the parent who could love her like I couldn't. He relented. I
drove away, with promises to call once I knew something.

It is here that I realize my car probably has enough
gas to make it to the filling station and no farther. Then,
another uneventful, short drive to the hospital, which is
where we are now, in the small room with the exterior
armed guard.

In my rush to get out of the house and due to my recent general dipshittedness, I'd neglected to grab something to do while I hang around the ER. Even on their
best days, emergency rooms are not known for their

lightning-like speed at handling cases that are not immediately life threatening, which is what I now am, since
the guard had been posted. This delay is as it should be,
of course. But, looking back, I realize that I didn't even
care that I had nothing to do but stare at the walls. So I
stare. Occasionally, I close my eyes in some vain hope
that I might fall asleep. I don't.

I also don't feel alone or lonely, really, just blank and
empty. One of this Catholic hospital's nuns pokes her head
in and asks "Oh, you poor dear! Is no one with you?"

"No," I say.

"Would you like me to sit with you?"

"You don't need to," I say.

"Would you like some coffee?" she asks.

"I'm fine," I say.

"A blanket?"

"No, thanks."

"A pillow, maybe?"

"Sure," I say simply because I feel like I should take
something from this wee helpful woman. "I might try to
catch a nap."

The nun—who is also locally famous for a series of
commercials with Peyton Manning, a local sports hero,
during which the nun plays basketball and football with
him—finds a spare pillow for me, then turns out a bank
of lights as she leaves. I still stare at the walls. Sleep
doesn't come. *Quelle* surprise.

A woman in a black dress swoops in and takes my
hand. I have never seen her before in my life. Before she
can explain who she is and why she is touching me, a
nurse comes in to keep me up to date on the hospital's
plan, which hasn't really taken shape yet. "Who are you?"
he asks. Great question, I think. "I'm her doula," the

woman says. But she's not—she doesn't look anything like my doula, in fact. I would swear on the grave of Kurt Cobain that I've never seen this woman before. I begin to wonder if my mental state is much, much more fragile than I'd believed. I don't say anything, just in case. The nurse leaves.

"I'm Toni," my doula tells me.

Toni? Who the heck is Toni? But I don't say anything.

"Cindy called me." Cindy was the doula who was at the baby's birth. "She couldn't get away but wanted someone here with you. Kimberly will be here shortly."

And, with that, my flock of doulas lands. For the next seventy-two hours, one of them would either be with me or on the phone with me whenever possible. It was, in a small way, like being gathered in angels' wings.

The nurse breezes back in to update Toni and me. There is no free bed in Tower 4, the Psych Ward, which is where all concerned are convinced I need to go. There is, however, a free bed in the normal hospital. The catch is that someone has to stay with me until I can be secured in the locked-down Tower 4. And I have to sign yet another large stack of papers, which promise that I won't be all sneaky and off myself while in the less-restrictive environment of a normal hospital. And if I do get past staff's watchful eye, attempt suicide, and survive, I promise to absolve the hospital of any responsibility.

There's just one problem with this whole plan: Scott has to be home with the baby. And we have no earthly idea who would be the best person to call in this sort of situation. We have no family closer than a six-hour drive. Our friends, while wonderful, have their own lives, besides which I don't want my friends to know that I'm not perfect, because they'd then stop liking me. Scott, who has been kept up to date by Kimberly, who has to keep leaving the hospital to use her cell, starts to call around. A tiny panic ensues, with Kimberly dashing between my ER room and the rain outside. Then Toni, bless her, offers to stay until we can figure it all out. "That is," she says, "if you don't mind."

Had my head been clearer—well, I wouldn't have been in the ER in the first place had my head been clearer—I would have hugged her. I start crying again instead. I don't deserve this kindness.

More paperwork and I am transferred upstairs to a regular hospital room, which is unlike any I'd seen before. It doesn't have its own separate bathroom. Rather, there is a small, camp-style toilet that flips out from under the sink. It's a wonder of engineering, all brushed stainless steel and clean enough to operate on, but nearly impossible to use unless you are under five feet tall or grew up in a dollhouse. The nurses urge me to take advantage of this elf-sized amenity so that I won't be inclined to leave the room sans supervision.

My first nurse, a student at the university, is barely old enough to drink. Whenever Toni has to step out to use the regulation-size restroom or make some calls, the nurse sits down to have forced conversations with me. She knows my name from my work at the newspaper. At first, I assume our chats are because she's just being polite or working on a research project. Then I realize that she's watching me, to make sure I don't do something tragic while my minder is away. Normally, I'm not paranoid, but after a couple of hours here, I know what it's like to live under Big Brother's thumb. This gets worse.

A comfortably round woman from Tower 4 comes in. Toni is asked to leave, which she does.

"Tell me what happened," the woman says. "What led you here?"

And so I go through it again. No harmony, still, and no catchy chorus.

"Any thoughts of hurting yourself?"

"No." I'm lying. What I should say is, "Not since I got here."

"Personal history?"

And so I tell her. Most of my teen years were pretty bleak but I didn't get any real help because I became very, very good at hiding it. I finally got some treatment when I couldn't get on a plane in my mid-twenties. Through hours of therapy, my shrink and I discovered the problem wasn't about the plane at all, but mostly a result of living with my mom, who had really come apart during my teen years and "wasn't able to help me develop any self-esteem," according to my student shrink. I'm still not certain how that related to flying, but the explanation gave me enough hope to pin some small faith in myself on my metaphoric chest. Later, that same shrink put me on Paxil after I showed up in her office one day, sobbing like I'd just seen my new puppy crushed by a semi, which I hadn't. The drugs had helped. I'd been off them for a couple of years and hadn't really had a problem. I wonder what that shrink would think of me now.

"Family history?"

And so I lay it all out. My maternal great-grandmother abandoned her kids, fell into a bottle, and was never heard from again. Most likely, she was bipolar, but no one has proof. My mother's mother hopped in and out of mental hospitals, then died very young from cancer. My mother's brother shot and killed himself after he got back from Vietnam. My cousin, after giving birth to her first baby, couldn't stop laughing and did some serious time in the Psych Ward. Oh, and my paternal grandmother darn near succeeded in killing herself when I was in college. I spent most of my adolescence living with my own mother, who was often not home, irritated at me, or sobbing in her bedroom for hours on end. Good times.

Then she says, almost smiling, "So it was really just a matter of time before you wound up here." This is only half a joke. Truer words have never been spoken.

During the rounds of phone calls that marked my admission to the hospital, some friends are rounded up and pressed into service. I suspect it's hard for them to really understand what's going on, because Scott and I are the first in our circle to reproduce. They don't know how much chaos that tiny lump of life can create. Plus, I don't want word of my psychological decline to get out, given how vicious Knoxville gossip can be. I know this because I've been too catty myself to believe that others are kinder than I.

I'd forgotten, however, that your true friends are friends no matter how strange your life may be at any given moment. Zak and Joey, the couple at whose wedding I figured out that I was pregnant, come over to our house to help Scott take care of the baby during that first night I'm away. Zak, a tall, blond TV producer with a wicked sense of humor, and Joey, a raven-haired, devastatingly beautiful and sensitive writer, stop at the Fellini Kroger on their way to pick up a can of formula that the baby needs. Also in the bag is a six-pack and some beef jerky. They settle in for the first shift.

Shelley, the one with the sane mother who reminds Steph and me of a zoo exhibit, takes the night shift in my hospital room so that Toni can get some sleep and a change of clothes. It's so good to see someone who knows what I used to be like before all of this that I start to cry again. Shelley, bless her, has gone to our house, rummaged through my drawers, and tossed a bunch of clothes in an overnight bag. In it, along with some clean underwear and a hairbrush, are the spring green floral pajamas that I'd initially bought to wear after having the baby. They seemed perfect for the Maternity Ward, cheerful and motherly. I even made sure they had a top with buttons on it, so that I could easily access my breasts. I had not got the chance to wear them, until now, where they just look wrong.

Shelley also flung in a copy of *Vanity Fair* magazine, just in case I want to look at big pretty pictures of celebrities while I recollect my marbles. We chat for a bit, about families and babies and brain chemistry. A nurse comes in to let me know that the doctor who has been assigned to me started throwing up and had to go home. I'll see him in the morning, she says, but first I have to take these. She hands me some pills and watches me swallow them. Shelley's voice drifts away and I sleep.

At some point during my stay in the regular hospital room, Toni the doula tells me that she wanted to know what I was like when I wasn't like this. She thought I was probably smart and funny, when I was in full command of my moods. "I am," I tell her. "I am a big hit at parties." But I don't mention all of the other stuff—how I don't know that I can ever be that person again, how I'm going to feel like this forever, how I can't live like this. And I don't mention how much I hate who I am, how I can't forgive people who hurt me yet love me, and how much I burn to be the radiant woman on the cover of all of the glossy magazines, the one who glows from the joy of having a new baby. I can't do this mom thing. I can't be perfect like that woman in the picture and I can never be perfect like her because of the chemicals in my brain and all this past history, which wrap around my ankles like quicksand and suck me down.

From my journal, July 13:

"The baby books don't prepare you for this, this wonderful event that can also lead to such angst and turmoil. I feel cheated somehow, as if I missed out on all of the cute bunnies and duckies of motherhood and got stuck with all of the poopy diapers. Part of me wanted your birth to be more celebrated, with all of the extended family throwing a big party for you and by extension (and selfishly) me. And it hurts to be so selfish. It's hard to let the spotlight rest solely on you. You deserve it, little one, but it is hard to admit that it is hard to no longer be the center of attention."

The next morning, as I'm waking up I think my father is visiting me, despite the fact that I know he is still in Ohio and not due to come to Knoxville for a few more days. As it turns out, the solid, balding, vaguely ethnic man sitting across from me is my new shrink, Dr. G. The resemblance fades after I wake up a bit more. Freud would have had a field day.

Dr. G, I later learn, is a Jew from Brooklyn and not, like my dad, an Italian from Pittsburgh. Briefly, before going to med school, Dr. G was a stand-up comic. People are interesting, even when you're not at your best. Dr. G opened his act by apologizing for not seeing me the previous night. I simply start to cry. It feels like I'm on the edge of a tall building, peering over the side at the pigeons circling below.

He does doctorly things like inquiring about my night's rest and how much I've been eating. He chitchats. I don't. He makes jokes. I don't laugh. Somewhere along the way, my sense of humor decamped for sunnier climes. He asks me to go through the chain of events again, then he gives me the medical headlines.

First bit of news is that I have a urinary tract infection, the first one I've ever had in my life, and the reason why I was having so many issues with my bladder. Insult, meet injury. It's probably the result of the catheter during the birth but it's hard to know for certain. I should be in more discomfort because of it, but am not because my pelvic nerves are still in a bit of a snit over the labor trauma. Simple UTIs can be cured pretty quickly, fortunately, with a course or two of antibiotics. The crying, however, is going to take a bit more time.

Second bit of news is that I officially have postpartum depression. Knowing that what I am feeling has a name is a strange comfort. My feelings are real and not just something I can get over with a Protestant backbone and a stiff upper lip. Dr. G mentions what every psychiatric professional brings up sooner or later. "You wouldn't tell a person with diabetes to just snap out of it. This is no different." If I had a quarter for each time I've heard this, I could pay for all the years of therapy.

Sad thing is, it's not true. Diabetes, at least Type I, lacks the stigma attached to mental illnesses. The public at large has no problem believing that a diabetic can manage her condition and live a fairly normal life. Once you've been diagnosed with a mental illness, however, you are suspect, as if any sudden movement could make you take a hostage and climb the clock tower. We are always on the verge of collapse, in the eyes of the inexperienced, and the media only helps to promote this idea with its wall-to-wall coverage of the country's Andrea Yateses.

As Dr. G puts it, I have "a disorder of mood rather than a disorder of thought." As of last night, I'm on an antidepressant called Remeron (aka mirtazapine), which also acts as a booster for the Zoloft, pushing it to work a little faster.

"Remeron will also increase your appetite and acts as a soporific, which is . . ."

"I know what 'soporific' means," I snap. It pisses me off that people assume the crazy are also stupid. "I'm a writer." I don't know why I'm compelled to tell him that.

"Oh," he says, and smiles. "What do you write?"

"I work for the weekly paper. I write about music and movies and books and people," I say. "I'm not the kind of writer who pens poems about her cats." Tears are still streaming down my face, yet I feel it's important that he know I'm not some sad, lonely little woman who dreams of being the next Emily Dickinson. It's weird when the ego butts in at inappropriate times.

"My son's in a band," Dr. G says. He gives me the name. I've actually heard of them and they have a small following in town. "You should do a story on them." It's a comfort to know that at least one of us thinks that I'll be back to my old life eventually.

The third bit of news is that I'm to be transferred to Tower 4 after dinner.

I pass the day with doula Toni and my *Vanity Fair*. Scott's mom is on a plane, heading back to Knoxville. The baby is spending another day in Scott's office, being cooed at by all of the women who work there. I am a worthless wife and mother. I don't know why Scott's stuck around all of these years. Oddly, this thought doesn't make me cry.

Shelley stops in after work. She's with me when the orderly comes in, pushing a wheelchair. She carries my bag as we weave our way through the bowels of the hospital, which wasn't so much coherently designed as randomly evolved. It's a maze down there. It's hard to tell one wing from the next when you are surrounded by white, waxed linoleum and clean white walls. The orderly confesses that he used to get lost a lot when he first started. Now he knows the routes well.

One last elevator ride and we are at the glass doors that separate the Psych Ward from the sane world. I'm wheeled through. Shelley surrenders my bag. The door closes. On the other side are Scott, his mom, and Shelley. Scott is holding the baby. I want someone to hold me, to touch me long enough to remind me that I'm human. They aren't allowed to visit tonight and can only wave through the glass. They all look terrified, like they've seen ghosts.

From my journal, July 12, evening, first night on the ward:

"Please get me out of here."

8

Like most healthy, mostly functional folks, my exposure to the inner workings of the average mental institution was limited to random media. I've seen *One Flew Over the Cuckoo's Nest* and *Nuts*. I may have read *Girl, Interrupted* at some point, but the only detail that stuck was the bit about the chicken bones under the bed. I also suspect that I saw an indie slasher flick set in an abandoned psych hospital, but, again, details are hazy. There may have been a chain saw.

In real life, I'd set foot on the property of such places only three times. In reverse chronological order and from most unthreatening to most threatening, I'll start with Lakeshore Mental Health Institute in Knoxville, a lush, hilly complex in one of the tonier parts of town not far from Knoxville's University of Tennessee. Lakeshore—technically on the shore of the Tennessee river, not a lake—has always been an active mental health facility that houses patients in its vaguely Gothic buildings. But, in recent years, it has opened up the campus to community members, building hiking and biking paths that are mobbed on pleasant days by southern ladies who lunch and moms with baby carriages. I'd walked the loop myself a few times, and it was always difficult to imagine that behind the locked doors of the well-kept buildings were actual crazy people, some of whom might be watching us enjoying the weather. The soccer field was always a chaos of kids and calmed any misgivings we might have had about being spied on. Surely kids wouldn't be allowed someplace unsafe?

Less innocuous, but still fairly unthreatening, was the Austin State Hospital, which, like Lakeshore, is a campus and not just a single building. It also takes up some prime city real estate and is about the same distance from Austin's UT as Lakeshore is from its UT. The State Hospital, during my Austin years, hadn't really embraced the idea of allowing the public unfettered access to the grounds, but it did allow some groups to use its community room for meetings. A theater company for which I occasionally stage-managed rehearsed in that big, white, vinyl-tiled space. We all viewed it as something of a lark, kismet that artists who were on the bleeding edge would rehearse near the lunatics. At least once during each and every show I worked, on a particularly frustrating evening when Melpomene had abandoned us for more fertile endeavors, someone would comment that it was time to check ourselves in.

According to my back-of-an-envelope calculations, adding up all the time I spent at the Austin State Hospital over the years would come out to three consecutive months of twenty-four-hour days on the grounds. If I had been a patient, it would have made a significant impression. But when you know that the guard at the gate will let you out when you drive past, you fail to notice the details of others' confinement. Only in hindsight do I remember the process of getting the community room key, which required producing some ID and being buzzed in and out of a security office every time. Looking back, I can remember how eerily quiet the grounds were most of the time, despite the fact that a significant population of people was locked behind closed doors. Then, I subconsciously chalked it up to the seasons—only fools would be outside wandering about during the hellishly hot Texas summers, springs, and falls. Now, however, it is slightly more sinister that the only people I ever really saw were those I knew who were directly involved with the company.

There was only one time when the reality of the location pointed itself out. During a rehearsal the phone rang. This was in the days before everyone and his dog had a cell phone, so the one phone in the community room was our only lifeline to the outside world. On the other end was a security guard, who advised us to stay inside the building and make sure the doors were locked. "Why?" I asked. "One of our patients wasn't around for bed check," security guy said, "and he can be a little dangerous."

They promised to call back when the rogue loon was buttoned down for the evening but never did. We all eventually ran to our cars en masse, giggling with anxiety and the thrill of the perceived danger. It was oddly fun, at the time. Now, I wonder what was going on behind the scenes. How much of a tizzy was the place in? I can only guess. Still, all of the doings at the state asylum were backstage to me. All I ever saw was the surface.

The most up-close and personal experience I'd previously had with a mental institution before my own confinement was just after my freshman year of college, when I was home for Christmas break. After my Dad and I had made the two-hour drive from school to his condo

in Pittsburgh, he gave me a few minutes to fling my bags
of dirty laundry artfully around my room, then asked me
to join him on the couch. This was unusual. Most of our
father-daughter chats happened in the car. Last time we'd
had a stationary discussion was shortly after I'd gotten
my first period. Both of us would rather have been swimming through a lake of hot lava than having that conversation about tampons.

This was different. For the first time, I noticed how
old my father had become while I'd been gone. What remained of his salt-and-pepper hair was now mostly salt.
He looked tired and somehow small.

"Your grandmother's in the hospital," he said. This
wasn't that shocking. She'd had a run-in with shingles
over the summer and had not made a swift recovery.
Then, the shoe dropped. "She tried to kill herself a few
weeks ago."

His voice dopplered out into mumbles.

Perhaps the only thing I will ever find appealing
about the second Gulf War is the phrase "shock and
awe." It unfolded in stages, my particular shock and awe.
The first stage was anger that no one had bothered to tell
me about the attempt until now. This is a bit of tradition
on both sides of the family when there is bad news. No
one wants anyone to worry about what might happen,
even if the circumstances are dire. I still wonder what
would have happened if my grandmother had actually
succeeded in offing herself. Would I have found out
about it when she didn't show up at the next family gathering? Oh, yeah, your grandmother's dead. Sorry. We
didn't want you to be upset. Have some pie?

While my righteous indignation was growing like
kudzu in a southern summer, the cognitive dissonance

set in. If I had to make a list of people I thought would attempt suicide, Courtney Love and almost any member of my mother's family would have been near the top. But my paternal grandmother would have been somewhere near the bottom, not far from Mother Teresa and Tom Hanks.

I don't mean to imply that my grandmother is saintly, just that taking her own life was out of character. Until that point, my grandmother was one of the few stable points from which I could navigate the adolescent seas. Every Sunday, we went to her house for dinner. Every Sunday, she and I would sit up in the kitchen and talk while the guys watched the Steelers or the Pirates or the Penguins on the downstairs TV. She'd tell me stories about the old neighborhood—by now, almost all of the family had moved out of the increasingly slumlike Brushton and into upscale Penn Hills/Churchill. She'd try to convince me to go to Mass. She'd tell me about growing up coveting peanut butter sandwiches because her mom would pack school lunches only with sausage and peppers or white pizza, foods that made it clear she wasn't an American. She told me about her mother, who died before I was old enough to know her. She'd try to teach me Italian, which I still don't speak. Sometimes, we just talked about school or my mom or nothing in particular while she made macaroni, meatballs and gravy, pasta "fazool," or manicotti.

I have never once referred to my grandmother as "Granny" or "Grandma" or, heaven forbid, "Meemaw." From the outset, she simply didn't answer if I called her something other than "Grandmother." I suspect that if I suffered some tragic accident, like falling down a well or something, she wouldn't answer my calls for "Grandmother" if I chopped off the last few syllables because I couldn't draw a full breath. My younger cousins can get away with "Grandma," which makes me peevish. As the first grandkid, I was the one who broke her in. They should thank me.

She has never been the archetypal grandmother, quick to kiss a skinned knee or forgive a broken vase. Instead, she's generally been a rigid hard-ass, although she has mellowed a bit as the years have passed. I escaped most of her wrath, because my parents and I spent the first nine years of my life living elsewhere. Still, she had her rules, even for me, the first grandbaby to grace that side of the family. During my first weeks of life, she visited my folks in Delaware. Unhappy, I suspect, with the general new baby chaos, she got both my mom and me on an old-school feeding schedule, where I got a bottle every four hours no matter what else was going on. Feelings about hunger were irrelevant. Order must be maintained.

My grandmother has also steadfastly refused to teach me how to cook, especially how to cook anything Italian. Her rationale was that I would go to college and hire a chef once the time came to forge out on my own. I wouldn't be stuck with long days of nothing but housework, like she was. Along the same lines, I wasn't supposed to get married because that would lead to kids, which leads to being trapped in the house. A good education would free me from the burdens of being female, which, to her, meant years of drudgery and boredom. She started lighting candles for me when I moved to Texas with Scott and was convinced that I'd made a huge mistake that only the Lord could undo.

Adults, however, truly bore the weight of her rules,

especially her two sons and stepkids. She clenched an iron fist around my dad's life when he was a kid, and she and my dad will always be at loggerheads. It got worse when my "blood" grandfather died when my dad was young. From that point on, fear drove my grandmother to new levels of Machiavellian machinations. It was she who decided that he'd go to Pitt to study engineering, because these choices were safe. He'd be close to home and guaranteed a decent job. My dad wanted to go away to study acting, but she refused to sign any of his applications. Family gossip swirls with allegations that she threatened him with either a wooden spoon or a chef's knife when he was insistent about doing his own thing. On the one hand, the image is hysterically funny. My father is a big, strong, barrel-chested guy, and was even more so as a teenager when he was working as a lifeguard. My grandmother is, on a good day, five feet tall and weighs less than a hundred pounds. On the other hand, it's profoundly sad. My dad has always been a firm believer in doing one's duty, no matter how unpleasant, but I wonder how it would have all turned out if he'd just turned his back on her demands and walked away. How different would his life have been?

My grandmother also picked my father's bride. That's overstating it a touch. She didn't pick my mother out of a mail-order catalog, but she was very specific about the type of woman my father was to marry. His bride would be, in her words, "white," which is to say that she wouldn't look Italian. My grandmother's only goal with this edict was that her grandchildren turn out white as well. In her eyes, there was no need to create another generation of dark, swarthy people who would always be marked as immigrants. It worked. My cousin Albert and I appear to have no particular ethnicity at all. But if you met our fathers, there'd be no denying our background.

Beyond that, she also had stringent household rules. No one was allowed to breathe in the living room, unless it was a major holiday and the house was full of people wanting to sit down. If mathematicians were allowed to examine the upstairs, they would have marveled at her ability to keep all of the Oriental rugs' fringe perfectly parallel. The upstairs bathroom, where my grandfather found her in a tub full of her own blood with slashes in both wrists and ankles, was only for baths. Showers were to be taken in the downstairs bath. The place was always immaculate. You could, if so inclined, eat off of the spotless garage floor. (This genetic quirk failed to find me. Sometimes, I'm not sure if we should eat off of our plates.)

The same unforgiving dogma ruled her personal life as well. Everything—from sheets to underwear—was neatly pressed. You could cut bread with the seams on her pants. Her hair was always done and her gray roots never showed. If she felt she was getting too heavy, she'd simply stop eating breakfast and lunch until she was back in fighting trim. With the perfect clarity of hindsight, it's no wonder that pictures never show her with a smile. I can't remember a time when she'd simply throw back her head and laugh.

Yet she wasn't distant, not with me, anyway. During the heat of my parents' divorce, I spent a few nights at her house. After a shower in, of course, the downstairs bathroom, I started crying. Because of some grandmotherly sense or very thin walls, she knew to come down and check on me. And for a good hour, we stayed down there. I, wrapped in a towel and sitting on the closed toilet. She, standing and holding my head on her shoulder. It is the most loved I'd ever felt until I met my husband.

That's what I'm thinking about as my father is explaining what happened that day in the tub in her house. He may have provided more details, but I was too busy processing how someone who seemed to have her life in such total control could ever be unhappy. But as a kid—even a college-aged kid—there's so much you don't see until you grow up and get some distance. If I recall correctly, I made some wisecrack as soon as my dad finished talking. A microsecond later I was apologizing for it, stammering that I didn't really know what I was supposed to say next. I still don't know. There is no formal etiquette for dealing with these sorts of things.

Instead, my dad and I stared at the television for a bit. He made a cocktail for himself and was sure to put a couple of maraschino cherries in the bottom of the glass. At some point, I reached over, fished them out, and ate them. It is one of our rituals. There is comfort in rituals.

That evening, we drove downtown to the loony bin where my grandmother was being kept. There are some sentences I never expected to utter in my life. That is one of them.

At this point, I'd love to write a nice long descriptive passage, where I paint photo-realistic word-pictures of my grandmother's hospital. But, back then I was still trying to wrap my head around what had happened and paid virtually no attention to where my dad drove. I want to say it was to Western Psych, but can make no promises. Suffice to say, it was downtown. We parked in a garage and walked a block or two in streetlamp dark to the hospital.

The images that come to mind now to describe the

ward itself can't possibly be real. My memory tells me that we walked through modern glass doors into a Gothic stone church, complete with flying buttresses and gargoyles. The nursing staff was out in the open at a modern-style reception desk. We had to wear stickers that identified us as guests. We were told where my grandmother's room was, then walked down long hallways lined with torches and tapestries. Other patients passed us, some wearing khakis and button-downs, others medieval robes. All are obviously mad.

We stopped just short of the end of the hall, where a huge day room featured a TV in the center with the volume up to 11. My grandmother's room was the same amalgam as the rest of the décor, with one sleek glass wall at the front and three stone walls on the other sides. A small, clerestory window was fitted with diamond-mesh reinforced glass. There were no curtains or sheets on the twentieth-century hospital bed. The ceiling was too far away to see.

I know this isn't real, but this is all my mind will let me remember.

My grandmother was unrecognizable. I'd expected her to be sitting primly on the end of her freshly made bed, fully herself in appearance and temperament. Instead she was pacing the tiny cell, wringing her hands like Lady Macbeth. She was wearing jeans, a sweatshirt with stains on it, and slippers. Her wrists and ankles were wrapped in gauze. What really blew the rest of my mind was her hair. Until that moment, I'd forgotten that my grandmother had gone completely gray in her early thirties. Her hair, as far as I was concerned, was always an auburn color. Now she looked like a punk rocker, long white roots with red ends. And she was talking, endlessly.

About nothing, really. I'm certain she didn't even know we were there.

Other family members wandered in. My stepaunt, who had great connections at the local hospitals through both her job and charity work, had a rundown of possible next steps. While she and my dad hashed through the options, I escaped outside and sat on the steps inhaling great gulps of cold December air. People passed on their way to somewhere fun or someplace safe. Eventually, my dad pulled up with the car. We drove home, but didn't speak much.

My holiday break passed quickly, which was a blessing. My favorite high school job, which was at a bookstore in the mall, still had need for me during that Christmas season. I took every hour I could get, simply so that I had something productive to do. Most nights, I'd just flop onto the couch, too tired to move. I visited my grandmother only once after the first trip. By then, she'd been transferred to a more traditional, suburban hospital, where the linoleum-lined rooms were sparkling white and fiendishly clean. Big windows looked out onto the parking lot and a tiny, snow-covered swath of lawn.

My dad and I stopped by shortly after she'd been for a shock treatment, which meant that she was groggy and confused. It was easier to take, somehow, than the manic babbling. Now she looked ill, like any other hospital patient who was receiving life-prolonging but exhausting treatments. I could pretend that she had cancer or heart disease, some kind of tangible disease that could be pointed to and blamed.

That's always been the biggest bugaboo with psychiatry. Until recently, there was nothing visible to pin it on,

other than ethereal theories about imbalanced levels of
black bile or demonic possession or lack of moral fiber.
Now, very, very tenuous inroads are being made into
what happens chemically and electronically in the brain
to cause mental illnesses. MRIs can show striking differences between a "normal" brain and one that is depressed. Serotonin and cortisol seem to be involved on a
molecular level, but no one's certain how. While these
theories are only slightly better than blaming bodily hu-
mors, their grounding in accepted clinical science makes
mental illness seem like more than the result of an over-
active imagination.

While we know precious little about the base causes,
we know even less about cures. For a few years at the
turn of the twentieth century, lobotomy was a popular
treatment, especially for "hysterical" women. Hacking
through a small part of the brain's frontal lobe did not
help the patient feel better, but it had the twin advantages
of making her not care about her madness while also
making her fairly docile.

Popular treatments midcentury were less grotesque
but not much better. As the country entered the age of
plastics, the "chemical lobotomy" of Thorazine offered
some hope to people with severe mental illnesses. Thorazine quelled suicidal impulses, but caused the patient
to shuffle, drool, and stammer. One psych nurse I met
during my very own stay in the nuthatch was old enough
to remember working the floor as a young nursing student, surrounded by vacant, twitchy patients who could
do little but stare. It's not surprising that most people
would rather be completely barmy than forced onto
drugs that strip the rest of their life from them.

The options are better now, even though researchers

still don't know exactly how most of them work. Modern pharmaceuticals are a heck of a lot more subtle these days and come in as many flavors as ice creams at a Baskin-Robbins. There are drawbacks, certainly. They are probably overprescribed because they are cheaper than other forms of therapy and are dished out even for the mildest blue mood. Most drugs do have some side effects, ranging anywhere from chronic cottonmouth to weird sexual dysfunctions. Still, for the truly ill, they can offer hope.

The biggest drawback to most therapeutic drugs is that they take so long to begin to work. Someone who is actively suicidal is as likely to wait three to six weeks for relief as a toddler is to eat a big bowl of broccoli and liver. Sure, it might happen. But the odds are greatly against it. This is where shock treatments (or Electroconvulsive Therapy, ECT, to be more politically correct about the nomenclature) can come in. ECT sounds just as barbaric as a lobotomy, and, on some levels, it is. The image of Jack Nicholson in *One Flew Over the Cuckoo's Nest* as he's getting strapped down and zapped like Frankenstein's monster is haunting—and it is a film I can never watch again. Actually, I can't watch it because of that and the fact that Danny DeVito, who could easily be my father's shorter twin, plays a character named Martini. *Cuckoo's Nest* will never be in my DVD player. It cuts too close to some barely scabbed-over wounds.

ECT proponents preach that it isn't just torture loosely described as therapy. The patient is given a short-acting cocktail of a sedative and a muscle relaxant and so isn't even vaguely conscious during the treatment. Two electrodes are placed on the head, usually on the temples and/or forehead. Up to a minute's worth of current passes through the brain to create seizures. The patient doesn't violently twitch or shake, however, because of the nice drugs. And that's it. Half an hour later, the ECT receiver is conscious, if a little bewildered. Although by the time your options include ECT, you're usually already bewildered, so it's hard to say which comes first.

The bitch of ECT is that it works. No one really knows why. It is counterintuitive medicine, certainly, and the first guy who tried it was the spiritual cousin of the first guy who ate a lobster. On some level, ECT is like chemotherapy, in which injecting poison into your bloodstream can be beneficial.

ECT isn't without side effects. Improperly done, it is brutal and can leave the patient stripped of most of his memory. Life is full of risks, however. Sometimes you have to just choose the ones you can live with.

Nonetheless, it is not easy to imagine my grandmother in a tiny, dungeonlike room, strapped to a metal table and repeatedly jolted with electricity. Even the realities of ECT are not the stuff of bedtime stories. But there was nothing I could do about it, other than brood, which I'd honed to a razor-sharp skill during my teen years. I bolted back to college as soon as break was over and flung myself into that life. There, I went to class (mostly) and studied (mostly), but I also found a place to escape. Deep in the bowels of the arts building was a theater. And in that theater were theater people, the geeks and weirdos and divas who enjoy pretending to be something other than they are in order to tell a greater story. This dank room could be transformed into an Edwardian garden or a sandy beach, far, far away from reality. The draw was magnetic.

I didn't tell anyone about my grandmother, even

when they'd ask about my break. There was too much stigma attached to spill the details. No one could possibly understand, no matter how many different ways I tried to explain it. And then I'd be marked as crazy, too, simply because of our relationship. I still snort at the irony of the whole thing, of being ashamed to tell my theater friends—most of whom have never been poster children for effective social adjustment—that I was related to real-life lunatics.

By the time my first year was over, my grandmother was back home. The first few times I went to her house to visit, she was anxiously flighty and unable to stay in one place. But she got better. She had therapy and drugs. She relaxed into her life in a way that I'd never have expected. She still kept her house immaculate, but her extreme rigidity was gone. Disorder wasn't her boon companion, but she could at least let it in the door, if briefly. We were able to sit in the kitchen and talk. Sometimes we'd even talk about feelings.

Would she have preferred that the whole thing had never happened? Sure. Everyone in the family would. I would prefer to look like Heidi Klum and live on ice cream. I'd prefer to have not had a breakdown after my child was born. Life as a whole really doesn't care what your preferences are.

Still, the changes my grandmother's episode wrought were largely good ones. Her memory isn't what it used to be, but it's hard to tell if that's a function of age or ECT. She is, however, alive. So there's that.

9

Disorientation, thy name is Tower 4.

Despite having lived a good thirty-plus years on this planet, a more heartbreaking moment than when the glass doors were locked behind me with my family stuck on the other side I've never endured. Yet the fact that this hurts so very, very much proves that I am not as far gone as I'd thought. It would have been nice to have my husband around to hold my hand for a few minutes, just to remind me that, in another life, I was human and loved. But sometimes cold comfort is all you can get.

I'm crying, of course. It's what I do now. It is my vocation. I should hire myself out to funerals as a designated mourner.

My bags, which include the suitcase that Shelley packed and my everyday work bag, are taken from me by a nurse. My work bag can't be classified as a purse. This L.L. Bean briefcase/security blanket is usually full of paper and pens, a microtape recorder, some gum, and other ephemera, like the card of the greatest cabbie in London and random phone numbers. Lately, it has included an overstuffed manila folder devoted to all of the paper that I've accumulated over the last two weeks, all of the insurance forms and the baby's birth certificate, for which I

keep meaning to find a safe place. Full of the documenta-
tion that I was a reasonable person at one point and all of
the mementos said reasonable person had accumulated,
this bag disappears into the nurse's station, a big glass fishbowl in the middle of the ward. It and my overnight bag
are searched while I am led away to complete still more
paperwork.

Describing the sensory assault of a psych floor can be
difficult, even for those in complete command of all of
their faculties. But this is what I recall: a short, dead-
eyed woman, who is so affectless that she could easily be
one of the patients, leads me down the hall for questions
while an older, badly sunburned woman wearing short-
shorts and a tank top, with ratted dyed-blonde hair, paces
around the perimeter of the nurses' station, muttering
nonstop under her breath. Even though I had a few
chemically induced hours of sleep the night previous, I
am exhausted. The place smells like stale fried chicken
and antiseptic. The fluorescent lights give everything a
greenish haze so that we all have the skin tones of 3 a.m.
Wal-Mart shoppers. We wind up in the "arts and crafts"
room, which is full of pipe cleaners, construction paper,
markers, and tape. She clears a space on the small round
table.

"What year is it?" Her voice never rises above a mon-
otone.

"2002," I say.

"What is your name?"

"Adrienne Martini," I say, and I start to launch into
my usual explanation that "Yes, it's just like the drink"
and "No, I'm not all that fond of them" but never get the
chance.

"How are your toileting habits?"

"Um, fine," I say. Years of social interaction have really not prepared me well for this day. And, for once, I don't launch into my usual spiel about using nouns as verbs and how adjectival phrases are abuses of the English language and must be stopped.

We move along to the written portion of the questioning, some of which I complete in green crayon until a pencil with a sharp point is located.

The forms seem pretty standard: name, date, previous mental illness, next of kin. Eventually, we come to the more creative part of this exercise. I have to complete sentences along the lines of "I would be happier if . . ." and "My main trouble is . . ." Later, one of the prompts tells me to "Write a complete sentence." I write "This is a complete sentence." My monotonatic minder smirks at my cheekiness. Finally, a breakthrough.

After completing this batch of paperwork—I continue to be amazed by how many trees must die for each patient I am handed off to another woman, a prim, gray-haired matron who wears reading glasses on a chain around her neck. She walks me to the other end of the hall, past a white board on which is written all of the patients' names, their room assignments, and, in big letters at the top, TODAY IS FRIDAY, JULY 12, 2002. It worries me that this needs to be announced, both to the staff and to the inmates.

We are sequestered in a bright little room that looks like it could be the office part of a well-worn hotel suite. This is also where I will meet with my shrink and my spouse, but I don't know that yet. It does, however, have a door that locks, which the gray-haired lady closes. She explains that she's a floater and that the psych floor isn't her usual rotation. Still, she admits, she does feel that she can do the most good in Tower 4, where the needs of the patients are obvious.

"What brought you here?" She sounds genuinely concerned with my plight, the first person in a while to do so. I go through the whole thing again.

"What was your life like before?"

I tell her. Good, mostly. I enjoyed my work and felt like I was doing something worthwhile. I explain that the whole baby thing took me by surprise, that I just expected it to be different, more fulfilling somehow. I stop crying. This is the first time I've admitted out loud that I am a defective mother and I've surprised myself. Plus, this woman seems to care a great deal, like she knows exactly how I feel and doesn't judge me for my imperfections.

"What church do you go to?"

I blink a few times. I don't remember this being part of the standard raft of questions. "Um, what?"

"What church do you go to?" She's smiling at me and nodding her head.

"I don't. I don't know that I believe in God."

"You're just too smart for your own good, you know," she diagnoses, with a grin. "Maybe that's why you're here. You should thank Him for what you have. And you should run a comb through your hair," she adds. I don't have the energy to explain that my hair always looks like this, regardless of my mental state. Besides, by this time, the reality of the situation has set in. I am on a Psych Ward. I am officially crazy. I deserve to be lectured on my failings. It's a lot to absorb on little sleep.

She goes on, but I've stopped listening. My mouth hangs open. These sorts of conversations are a matter of course in Knoxville, where you can't perform a Satanist

ritual without hitting a Baptist church. In any other cir-
cumstance, I could have just walked it off. But, now, I
burst into tears, like a balloon pricked by a needle. A certain level of hell is reserved for those who proselytize to
those over whom they have power.

If I could have left, I would have. And that is the rub
of Tower 4: You are no longer in control of your hospital
stay. Other people, some of whom also seem to be of
questionable sanity, control your comings and goings.
The doors are locked and only those in the little glass
booth have the keys. Even someone who is generally not
very paranoid, like, say, me, finds herself second-guessing
everything she says. After a few days, your speech becomes littered with hesitations; moments where you re-
think every last word and scan it for any possible
misinterpretations. If you weren't already slightly mad,
this would pack you up and drive you to its borders.

We finish the forms, I think. I've stopped paying attention to what she's saying and answer in monotones.
I'm sure somewhere on that form is a note that I'm "un-
responsive" and "hostile" and "too smart for my own
good." Fuck it.

I'm handed back over to the first woman for a tour of
my new home away from home. Tower 4 is shaped like a
racing oval, with the aforementioned glassed-in nurses'
station in the center and patient rooms, activities rooms,
a day room, phones, and a few offices around the
perimeter. The "Recreational Therapist" would later inform us that eighteen laps around the floor measures out
to be a mile.

There are twenty-four patient beds, two to a room.
Women outnumber men by about two to one. Anonymity
is prized on the floor. Patients are given a code number

and no incoming calls or visitors will be allowed unless the other person has this code. The staff will neither confirm nor deny the presence of anyone asked for by name. On some levels, this is comforting. No one need know of my time here unless I disclose it. But it's double-edged: Keeping this a secret makes it more shameful, and there is already enough shame attached to depression. However, without this promise of facelessness, some who desperately need help wouldn't take this first step to get it for fear of having it made public. And so the sword cuts again.

In each room are two dressers, a mirror, at least one comfy chair, and a corkboard on which flyers about how not to fall down are tacked. In most ways, these look like traditional hospital rooms. What's striking is what's missing, like IV stands, TVs, and all the other clutter that crowds the room of a physically sick person. The mentally ill person's room looks like a cheap European motel room, stripped of all mod cons, save that the bed is higher tech and it has a private bathroom. Everyone walks around in street clothes, rather than hospital garb, which makes it even harder to tell staff from patient.

My bags have been thoroughly searched. I have to sign off on the contraband that has been found so that it can be locked away for the good of us all. Simple things like keys and cash are verboten, as is aspirin and an elderly Paxil wedged in the crevasses of my work bag. Also confiscated is my hair conditioner, which contained trace amounts of alcohol and could be abused by some desperate drunk. The staff would ration out appropriate amounts before each shower. At least I get to hang on to my clothes, the red leather journal, and some books, all of which are delivered to my room while we continue the tour.

The last stop is the TV room, a cavernous space with

couches, a pool table, assorted puzzles, a big box of crayons, and some coloring books. There is also an attached kitchenette, where the refrigerator is always stocked with juice boxes, milk, fresh fruit, and ice cream. All of this we are encouraged to eat at will, which one of the patients does unceasingly, plowing through cup after cup of ice cream whenever her eyes are open. The TV is almost always tuned to Great American Country, because one of the patients gets all worked up if you change the channel.

I meet my roommate, Sandra, who is maybe in her late-thirties and has the same sort of uncontrollable frizzy hair that I have been cursed with. There are dark circles under her eyes and her wrists are covered in stitches. She also carries around a plush baby doll that giggles and coos whenever you press its hands. Sandra and the nurse seem keen on my seeing this. I want to run because it's just so creepy, especially when it starts to make those almost lifelike noises and writhes. I'm introduced to other patients, but the information fails to stick. Terror sinks in.

It's hard to pinpoint exactly where this terror springs from; perhaps it is simply because they are overtly friendly and I'm trying to remain aloof. For someone whose limbic system is already maxed out, it's impossible to come to grips with this place and its denizens. I don't belong here. I don't want to be here. I want to go home, to my own bed, where everything failed to make sense in a more predictable way. I want to go back to my life before all of this happened.

We finish the tour. I wander back to my room, where I hide, balled up on the bed, crying, until it is time for group.

*   *   *

Before we go further, let me make note of one important
thing. While I did not believe it at the time, Tower 4 was
exactly where I needed to be. It is one of the safest places,
physically and emotionally, I have ever experienced. My
stay is both something I'm glad to have had and something
I never want to do again. Everyone, mentally healthy or
no, could benefit from spending some time up there.

Each Tower 4 guest is given a schedule of daily activities,
not unlike guests at a very nice spa, but without hot stone
massage or fruity health tonics. Since I came in at the
end of the day, the only thing I am expected to do is attend the nightly group wrap-up, where every patient
must tell the group how the day went. All new people, I'd
discover, always do the same thing, which is sit in the
back of the room and try to remain invisible. I am no exception. I also cry the whole time. You'd think I'd be hor-
ribly dehydrated.

Group therapy on Tower 4 is a remarkably nonlinear
affair. Of the two dozen people on the floor, most of them
are suffering from a disorder of mood rather than one of
thought. The mood people, while alternately glum or
manic, can carry on a basic conversation, even if they are
twitchy or sobbing. However, the other folk—those with
disorders of thought—make this nightly exercise full of
sudden diversions, roundabout progress, and the occasional low-hanging branch. During evening group, each
patient must declare whether or not the goals set at
morning group had been achieved. Not being there for
the morning group, I only had to introduce myself and
explain briefly why I was there, but only if I felt comfortable doing so.

Perhaps one of the most refreshing things about Tower 4 is that very little is mandatory. Share if you feel comfortable. Get out of bed each day. Eat when you can. Have your vitals taken twice daily. And attend the day's groups, which can range from recreational therapy (better mental health through leisure activities) to mindfulness (better mental health through meditation) to drug information (better mental health through chemistry).

Behavior that would attract scorn in the outside world isn't even remarked upon during groups on the psych floor. Polite fictions abound. A woman wrapped in a hospital blanket dips in and out of consciousness. Another moans for forty-five minutes, then wanders off. Whenever the conversation really gets rolling, someone never fails to veer back into nonsense-land.

That night's social worker, who looks like a male high school science teacher complete with a cardigan sweater, starts us off by talking about goal setting. He gets in about two sentences before being interrupted by a black-haired squatty woman in a wheelchair. "I ain't brain broke," she says. "My son says I'm brain broke, but I ain't."

"I hear you, Vivian. We're talking about goals right now," the social worker says in a voice that radiates calm.

"Okay. But I ain't brain broke."

If I didn't know better, I'd say the more obviously functional of the assembled lunatics rolled their eyes. That could have just been my imagination.

A fair number of patients lounge on the three couches near the TV; others pull up chairs on the perimeter. The sunburned woman paces around the perimeter, still mumbling to herself. Every now and again, she'll go over to the pool table and roll around some of the balls. No one pays her much attention.

There is one patient, however, who seems to set everyone off. Angola is one of those hardworking Appalachian women who have been ill used by life. She's raw boned and tall. About sixty, if I had to guess. Half the time it's hard to tell if she's actually completely crazy or just acting completely crazy. She sings old hymns throughout group, sometimes so loudly that the social worker has to shout over the choruses to be heard. If life were more poetic, her voice would be gorgeous and serene. Instead, it is nails-on-a-chalkboard screechy, the kind of noise that convinces you that Norman Bates is sneaking up from behind.

The social worker goes around the room and asks each patient if he or she had accomplished the goals set during the morning group.

"Jeff, you said that you wanted to write a letter to your ex-girlfriend. Did you?"

"Nope," Jeff declares. "I did finish a puzzle."

"Myra, you were going to call your mother."

"I've decided to just live one day at a time," Myra says. "See, thinking about the future is what got me here. I just want to live in the 'now.'"

"Rose, your goal was to make a plan for the day you are discharged."

"I just read these articles about drinking more red wine. I think more red wine would be good for my heart. What do you know about red wine?"

And on it goes.

Eventually, we get to me.

I sputter out my name and "postpartum." It's all I get out before I'm crying so hard I can't really breathe. I used to give talks to college kids and writers' groups. Now, I can't even say my name and condition. Humility is never a pretty lesson to learn.

One mousy, heavyset girl catches my eye. "I went through the same thing when my first was born," she says, sincerity ringing in her quiet voice. "You'll get through it."

It is a small comfort.

After group, I call Scott and beg him to get me out of here. "I don't belong here," I plead, desperate to get away from all of these crazy people. They are all so strange and emotionally unpredictable. I'm not like them. I'm just so sad and tired. I don't get the irony of this thought until much later.

Scott agrees with me, but there is little he can do, given that it is now almost 8 p.m. and those who can make decisions left the office hours ago. I assure him that my shrink will see the errors of his ways and turn me loose the next morning.

Over the phone, we agree to not tell my mom. First, I don't think I'll be locked up long enough to have it be a real issue, given that I'm convinced that I'll be leaving in the morning. Second, I just don't want to deal with her right now. I know that the first words out of her mouth will be "I told you this would happen if you didn't let me help you."

We assure each other of our undying love, despite the fact that one of us is crazy. The baby is well. Since Scott's mother is back in town, he has help. I can do nothing else right now except sleep. And with the help of an Ambien, doled out by a nurse upon my request, the rest of the first night passes painlessly. A few years ago, the option of pharmaceuticals on demand could have been a fun little experiment. Now, I'm just ashamed that I'm a failure at something so simple as sleeping.

*   *   *

From my journal, July 13:

"One of the best views of Knoxville is from the window of room 412 of St. Mary's Hospital Psych Ward. From here, I can see how the city is sunk into the valley. The Eastern European-esque tower block of student housing rises on the far left, blotting the bowl of mountains with its concrete ugliness. On the far right are the Fulton High School football fields. If I crane my neck a bit, I can see my favorite tennis courts.

"From my seat, one-eighth of the view is mountains and city. The rest is sky. Gray clouds hang. It's rained on and off all day, leading to yet another power outage. There was a ruckus of the staff rounding up all of the patients in the half-light.

"Some oddities about the Psych Ward:

"No trash can liners.
"The window blinds are sandwiched between the
    panes of reinforced glass.
"Being a non-smoker really cuts down on your
    chances to socialize. Every hour, the smokers
    cluster in front of the nurse's station where
    they are given one cigarette and herded to
    the smoking room.
"Generally, the night staff is a heck of a lot more
    fun than the day staff.
"It is a lot like what you'd see in the movies."

I'm being a bad, bad girl and hiding in my room. Technically, I'm accomplishing one of my goals—journal writing—which I'd set in group that morning. Every fifteen minutes, an orderly sticks his head in and marks my location on a chart. Twenty-four hours a day, a staff member wanders around making sure that we can all be located. It has been noted by him that I am not out bonding with the group. To be honest, I've never really been much of a joiner, sane or no.

It started with breakfast. My roommate, who is actually very nice, gives me a nudge so that I don't miss it. We pad down to the day room in our jammies and slippers. I'm still wearing the green florals, which draw compliments from both patients and staff. They tell me I look very cheerful.

At breakfast, I take the only empty seat, which is right next to Angola. A nurse sits on her other side, reminding her to take small bites. It does no good. She shoves all of the oatmeal in her mouth at once, chokes, then runs to the trash can and pukes. It's a great way to start the day. On top of that, I'd swear my coffee has no caffeine in it.

We have to stay in the room until we have our vital signs taken, our lunch orders filled out, and our trays examined. I am told that I've eaten only about 10 percent of my eggs and bacon. It is marked on my chart.

"Don't get the chicken," Myra whispers to me, just as I'm about to mark it on my lunch order.

Sandra and Jeff concur. "It fucking sucks," Jeff says. He's a man of few words, that Jeff, a sage for our times. The four of us chat like old friends, talking about group last night (I was right about the eye-rolling) and about the other patients. I am warned that Vivian, the one in the wheelchair, steals stuff from people's rooms. I discover that while I was doing my sleeping beauty the previous night, the big guy who didn't talk much had a total meltdown and it took four orderlies to get him sedated. Apparently, furniture was thrown.

When we're finally released from the day room, Angola is running up the hallway, naked. A nurse is chasing after her and the hospital gown in her hand flags out behind her. She is pretty spry, that Angola, even if time has not been kind to her backside. Conversation halts. We each walk by the nurses' station, collect our Dixie cups full of pills, and go about our morning business.

I take a shower, which is uneventful but for the realization that the showerhead is handheld so that no one can strangle himself by looping a wound-up bedsheet or something over it. Yet, we are still given potentially lethal motorized beds. The world is inconsistent, even here.

Morning group goes as one would expect. One aging southern belle is wrapped in a blanket in her chair, moaning and sobbing so hard that snot runs down her upper lip. Jeff points out to the social worker in charge that she's getting worse, that yesterday she was coherent. The social worker tells Jeff, essentially, to worry about his own health. I set one goal, which is to write in my journal. I'm pulled out of group by my shrink, who takes me to the cheap hotel room where the prim lady tried to lead me to Jesus.

"How's it going?" Dr. G asks, peering over the edge of his reading glasses.

"Fine, except for the woman who tried to get me to pray with her." I tell him the whole story. I have no idea if he believed me or if he just thought I was also delusional and looking for excuses to be angry about this place.

"Did you tell her to just stick it?" He's very direct, that Dr. G.

"Um, no. I didn't know I could." And I didn't. I keep forgetting that I'm an adult.

"You can. How are you otherwise?"

"I'm fine," I say. "And I want to go home." I don't, really, but I do want to be someplace where people don't vomit at breakfast.

"You're not ready to go home." And, with that, I burst into tears again, at which point, some small part of my brain notices that it has been almost twelve hours since I last cried. It's a minor miracle.

"But I don't belong here," I say. I don't. I've been to college. I am a professional; I write. I've read *Infinite Jest*. Twice. And understood it, which ought to count for something. I am too smart for this place. I'm not like them, those sad, crazy people out there.

"You do belong here," he says, then goes on to explain in great detail that he won't keep me here one minute longer than absolutely necessary, that psych-floor beds are in great demand, and that he wouldn't waste one on someone who didn't need to be there. He continues, but I've already started insisting that I'm just fine, thanks, now let me out of here. And he again says no.

Then I'm dismissed. The whole meeting took about five minutes. I feel like I'm just being warehoused, here, that no one really wants to talk to me about how I'm adjusting to any of this. I'm just here because no one knows what to do with me because I am brain broke. Dr. G and I would repeat this little exercise every morning of my confinement save the last, when I finally admitted that I might have a bit of a problem re: the whole mood stability issue and probably do belong on Tower 4. That day, I am released.

But I am getting ahead of myself.

When the door opens, I go to my room to hide. I write for a while, then read a few chapters from David Sedaris's *Me Talk Pretty One Day*, which Shelley had also tossed in my bag. I suspect it would not be on the approved reading list for the mentally ill.

From my journal, July 13 (later):

"Deep down, I think this whole thing was triggered by the dark fear that I'll be a crappy mom. I honestly don't know how I can escape that. I am a product of crappy mothering myself. Scott seems to have absolute faith in me. I wish I shared it.

"I just want to do the whole parenting thing right— and I know there is no such thing, really. But I feel I should at least give it the best shot. I got a little lost in it, though.

"Part of the problem is that I'm not really sure if I love *you* yet. I mean, I love the idea of you and the you you will become, but right now you're just a crying, pooping ball of need that threw my life out of control. The irregularity of you—you have your own arcane inner schedule that neither of us has been able to decode—can be a little tricky to accept on a daily basis. You seem alien at times, speaking a language and living in a world we can't see or comprehend. And at 4 a.m., you feel that much more foreign to me and I wonder how I could understand so little about something that used to be a part of me. I feel inferior and inept at something I should be a natural at. The whole pregnancy and birth thing is by far the hardest thing I've done. Usually hard projects bring great rewards. But right now, there hasn't been a great payoff, which makes it hard sometimes to soldier on."

The rest of the days were oddly similar to my first so I can't tease one out from the next. Sandra, Myra, Jeff, and

I chummed around, mostly because we seemed to have the same psychiatric issues. Sandra and I would have comfortable chats in our room, frequently before drifting off to sleep, like two girls at a slumber party. We'd gossip about the nurses, about our fellow patients, about the meds we were on. While we'd mention family—she had a daughter who was pregnant—our outside lives really didn't exist. She never really wanted to talk about the specifics of why she slashed her wrists, which was fine. I can imagine quite well without needing a full description. Sandra never pried too deeply into what brought me in, either. I suspect that she understood on a visceral level, in a way that most people couldn't.

Myra was hard to get a read on. She seemed like your average suburban young adult in her early twenties. Her parents would drop off copies of *Teen People* and *Elle*. She could name all of the members of the current hot boy bands. But the circles under her eyes were so dark, you'd swear she'd been punched. And she'd giggle a lot, and never when something actually amusing would happen. It's like she wasn't completely present, that some part of her was always floating just above her head in a helium balloon.

The amount of medication in Myra's morning and evening Dixie cups was truly astounding. While we did have to swallow our drugs in front of the nurse's window, the more trustworthy among us were allowed to collect our cups and loiter outside of the staff's fishtank. I made some offhanded comment about how the color of my drugs clashed with the energy of the room and that it was offensive to the building's feng shui. Myra giggles hysterically. "How do mine fit?" she asked.

"You have a rainbow, which is a positive sign," I say.

"You are so funny! That's what I've always liked about you."

Even crazy, I still got it.

Jeff seemed like the sanest of all of us, frankly, yet he'd been there long before I'd arrived and would remain long after I left. He reminded me of a singer/songwriter friend of mine. They have the same build, and the same vocal timbre and accent. It was weird to talk to Jeff, simply because if I closed my eyes, I could easily forget where I was. His voice could instantly transport me to my favorite bar, where I could have a beer or two and listen to great music, just like normal folk.

Jeff and I did a lot of jigsaw puzzles, simply because they don't require that much concentration and give you a sense of accomplishment. Of course, we couldn't finish any of them. Over the course of many, many patients, most of whom were not exactly paragons of responsible behavior, a lot of the pieces had disappeared. It was maddening to run out of bits and still have a big white hole in the middle of your pastoral mountain lake or pristine New England fishing village. Still, it was something to do.

One afternoon, over an autumn country road and a basket of kittens, Jeff asked if I wanted to know why he was here.

"Sure," I said, "but only if you want to tell me."

"I threatened to kill my ex-girlfriend and her new husband. Jesus told me to do it."

"Good to know," I said. And left it at that.

Apart from jigsaw puzzles, reading and writing are the best ways to fill the free time that floats around the Psych Ward like a mugger looking for a victim. Free time can lead to too much thinking; not that thinking is bad, per se, but too much of it is a lousy thing when you're already clinically blue. I get through all of Sedaris and most of a book of science fiction short stories. When I finish the Sedaris, I hide it on a bookshelf in the day room, wedged between two nondescript self-help paperbacks. As far as I know, it's still there.

I also take my meds, which comes with a matching set of mental baggage. I hate them. Over the years, various licensed professionals have tried to soften the ego blow of antidepressants. I don't care. Despite all of our warm and fuzzy talk about how depression is a physical disease caused by a chemical imbalance, it still has a big stinking stigma attached to it. If I could just mass my will behind it and decide to be happy, I wouldn't have to lean on a chemical crutch. Because I can't, I take my drugs like a good little girl. They help, damn it. While they aren't happy pills that make your heart sing, they do make everything just a little bit easier.

Most doctors want to see that your meds have kicked in before you are released. I can't exactly put my finger on when I started to feel better. My second night on the floor, I sleep soundly without any medical intervention. Twenty-four hours into my stay I can get through complete sentences without sobbing. A couple of days in, other patients stop asking me if I am okay. No one moment marks the turning point. It takes weeks before I can actually take naps again, however.

Different members of the staff would interview me every couple of hours. Questions range from those about my family history to my future plans. Some of the interviewers are fun. A nurse and I drift off onto a tangent about what it was like in the old days, when ECT and seriously unsubtle pharmaceuticals were the cutting edge of psychiatric therapies. One social worker, who I could easily imagine burning her bra in the seventies, told me that she liked me and that I would be just fine. I chose to believe her.

I also spend some time coloring, just like I used to do in first grade. "Piglet and Pooh in an Umbrella" is one of my favorite creations. It is a delicate work done in crayon and marker. Some day, I will give it to my child and say "This is what I did during your first month of life."

We watch rented movies some nights. Nothing too violent, of course, since the staff has to clear the film before it can be shown. I suspect *One Flew Over the Cuckoo's Nest* would be verboten, as would *Nuts*.

Scott and the baby come by every day. We are allowed to lock ourselves in the same room where I meet with my shrink. The visits are both too brief and too long—and still painful to talk about. Seeing my husband is wonderful. Seeing my daughter is not. Here is this crying, cranky thing who has ruined my carefully constructed life. I don't feel much connection to her at all and I know that I am truly defective. At the same time, I have never seen anything more beautiful, which makes it seem impossible that she has come from me. All I can say is that, now, I love her so much it is impossible to quantify.

I start to get really tired of fluorescent lighting, air conditioning, my green pajamas, and country music.

My dad flies in. He and my mother-in-law divide up the duties. Char takes care of the baby while he takes care of the cleaning. Each plays to his or her strengths. One night, Dad, Scott, and the baby come up bearing a piece of homemade lasagna, salad, and garlic bread. The staff, jokingly, threatens to confiscate it. I, jokingly, threaten to stab anyone who tries. And, thankfully, they take it for the light humor it is and don't immediately put me in restraints. It was the best lasagna ever. A week of hospital food makes you appreciate the wonders of the home oven.

My dad looks deeply uncomfortable the entire time, like he's hovering between crying and running. I'm sure it brought back memories of visiting his mother. It doesn't help that during his whole visit, the sunburned woman circles the table, muttering, and Angola is singing hymns as loudly as she can. I don't really notice them anymore, but my father must have wondered how his daughter ended up surrounded by the obviously mad. It's one thing when it happens to a parent; it's completely different when it happens to your child.

His reaction sums up the reasons I don't want anyone else to visit me. My writer friends would simply sit silently and take notes, while they were secretly creeped out by the more flamboyant patients. Everyone else would look at me with pity. I'd have to get a new set of friends, if they came here. From that moment on, I would be associated only with Angola, Vivian, and the sunburned woman.

Life on the ward continues. There are staff-designed distractions. The recreational therapist leads us on walks around the floor, with the more able-bodied continually lapping those who are more easily distracted. Angola makes it one lap, then starts to strip off her clothes. It feels just like home.

Later that day, a group of nurses leads the assembled lunatics in what is, quite possibly, the most surreal activity I've ever taken part in. We are handed a list of seventeen scrambled words and given fifteen minutes to figure

them out. The scrambled words are all names of medications we might be on. See if you can play along:

OOLIKNNP =

ITIUMLH =

DKAOEPTE =

As we're beavering away, the disorder-of-thought
folks are wandering about the room, some flapping their
papers like wings.

I also spend the days attending group. If nothing else,
group provides a benchmark for what crazy truly is. But
group offers more than that. No one can better understand where your head's at than someone who has been
there. No matter how down you may be, your words can
still offer succor to someone further down than you. Listening to other people, no matter how nuts they appear,
is worthwhile. The group-therapy experience should be
made into a feel-good movie with Robin Williams, but
that doesn't make it any less true. The advantage to my
group experience is that Knoxville is a large enough city
to have segregated Psych Wards for different sorts of con-
ditions. The truly violent are kept elsewhere, as are recov-
ering addicts of all stripes. Speaking only in terms of
*loco*ness, Tower 4 contains a fairly homogenous group.
There are no father-stabbers and mother-rapers, to quote
Arlo. We're all just fruits and nuts on this Group W
bench.

Sandra is the first to leave the nest. On the morning
of her release, she is sitting on the edge of the bed staring
at her wrists. "I just don't think I can do it," she says, quietly. "I just don't know that I'm ready to go back out
there. I'm so scared that it'll get worse."

I have no panacea. All I can say is that I'm terrified, too. Staying here forever would be worse, though, so we have to make a choice. We wander down to the TV room, where group is about to begin. When it's Sandra's turn to speak, she spills out her fear. We all make commiserating noises. The recreational therapist then leads us in a round of Pictionary and gives us words like *golf* and *sewing*. For a group of people who have to be told what day it is, I think we kicked some Pictionary ass.

At lunch, Sandra's daughter picks her up. I hope Sandra is still okay.

10

The morning of the day of my return to polite society begins like any other. Breakfast with Angola is invigorating, to say the least, but there is no puke during this repast. One of the new guys—he'd been on the floor for two days—is complaining that the kitchen staff is out to get him. "I keep ordering two eggs and three pieces of bacon," he yells. "What I get is oatmeal!" No matter how many times an aide explains to him that he is on a doctor-ordered low-cholesterol diet, he still blames a vast kitchen conspiracy, dreamed up just to torture him.

Myra and Jeff want to know every last detail about my new roommate, who was delivered last night just after dinner. I don't have much to tell them. She has been sound asleep every time I wander into the room. I know she must be conscious occasionally; I saw some chicken bones, all that remained of her dinner, left on a tray in the room right before I went to bed. She reeks of cigarette smoke, is a good-sized woman, and prefers to sleep without underwear, which I had bracingly discovered that morning after she'd kicked off all of her sheets. Some things you just don't want to know about strangers.

After a bowl of Cheerios and some coffee—we are all convinced there is a vast kitchen conspiracy to pass decaf off as the real thing—I wander to the nurse's fishbowl to collect my meds and some hair conditioner. I return to my room. My new roommate is still asleep, but more modestly covered. I take a shower. After so many days on my body, which is still leaking sweat and blood with abandon, my cheerful green jammies are begging to be washed. I ponder bagging up some dirty clothes for Scott to take home the next time I see him.

My fellow mental patients, those who can set goals, and I gather for morning group. Vivian still takes great pleasure in reminding the assembled that she isn't brain broke, no matter what everyone says. I make a mental note to warn my new roomie about Vivian, whom I've caught twice rolling into our rooms on little cat wheels to steal things. I happened to be there reading and once I found her with her hand in my luggage. In truth, there's not much of value for her to take, but it's still irritating. And, for the record, she, indeed, is not brain broke, but likes everyone to think that she is more disabled than she is.

My goals for the day are fairly straightforward. I need to finish up my discharge paperwork, which includes a "Crisis Intervention Plan" for which I have to list the names and phone numbers of people I can call in case of emergency as well as my five "early warning signs" of an impending breakdown. It's not a project that requires a great deal of effort on my part. I actually know five people I could call in an emergency. It's not as easy for others, however. It's hard to say if the mental illness has destroyed their social networks or if really bad social networks fostered the mental illness. Some patients never have visitors. I can imagine few things more lonely.

My real, if unstated, goal, is to finish reading a book of science fiction short stories that I'd just started. Even before the baby, my life didn't contain much unstructured time for reading. Three days ago, I didn't understand how much of a blessing this was. Now that I can stop crying and actually focus on something, I'm hoarding the minutes that I can spend with my nose in a book.

"You could spend some of the time writing about what brought you here," the social worker suggests. He's a good guy. We've spent some time outside of group just talking about our lives in the outside world. He is close friends with one of the best-known writers in Knoxville, whom I also work with. "I hear you're a bit of a writer." He winks at me, then, and smiles.

Dr. G pulls me out of group.

"How are the moods?" he asks, peering over the top of half-glasses.

"Okay," I say, then realize that it's true. While I feel light-years away from my old self, I do feel more stable than I have in weeks. I can get through massive chunks of time—five or six hours—without breaking down. It is an accomplishment.

"How is the sleeping?"

"I can sleep at night, thanks to the Remeron. But I still can't nap. I lay down yesterday in the hope that I could sneak in a nap but nothing worked."

He nods at me and asks about home. Is there help there?

I tell him there is. My mother-in-law and dad are still in town and will be for a bit.

"Do you want to go home?"

"Sure," I say. But I'm not certain that I mean it. The idea of home is appealing, yet I'm not sure I can handle the reality of it. I mention this.

"You can always come back if you need to," he says.

And it surprises me that I find this comforting, that a return to this place could be preferable to my own house.

I call Scott, who makes plans to come and fetch me at noon. I pack my stuff, including the green pajamas that I will never wear again. I turn in my paperwork, collect prescriptions for my meds, and make the required follow-up appointments. I kill time by working on a puzzle with Jeff. We finish it as best we can, given that there are still so many pieces missing. This is not a metaphor. We're both irritated that we can't complete something so banal and grouse about it. I vow to deliver a bunch of unopened puzzles to the ward as soon as I can.

The Hub shows up promptly at noon. I sign for my personal belongings and am buzzed out. Everyone waves as I go, like the staff at a particularly friendly hotel.

As we're riding the elevator down to street level, Scott asks how I feel. Terrified, I tell him. I'm not sure if this was the answer he expected, but it is the blunt truth. I am terrified. What makes me think I can do this now, when I have failed so spectacularly at it in the past?

After so many days in climate-controlled comfort, walking into the heat is like walking into a preheating oven. It feels good at first, because it's such a novelty. Then it's just hot. Scott loads my bags into the car, which doesn't feel like mine anymore. We drop off my prescriptions at the pharmacy down the hill, drive the five minutes to our humble house, and pull into the driveway. I'd forgotten how dumpy it is and notice every loose shingle and cobweb. The daylilies, however, are in spectacular bloom, a riot of orange and red and pinks. I love a plant that can thrive despite extreme neglect.

Our next-door neighbor, whose blonde wig and red lipstick are often askew, pops her head over the fence.

Hymns blast from a nearby radio she always plays when working out in the yard. When she found out we were going to have a baby, she was more excited than my own mom. During the last few days, Scott has caught her sneaking up to our front door and peering in so that she can catch glimpses of the baby. It is more funny than threatening. "Where have you been?" she demands. I want to tell her the full truth but don't. "I had some health problems," I say. "But I'm back now."

Scott unlocks the back door for me—I can't figure out what I've done with my keys since I've been crazy—and we stroll in. I don't know what I'm supposed to do now. Neither does anyone else, it seems. My dad and I hug awkwardly. My mother-in-law hugs me, too, then rattles on about how the last few days have been. She's talking extra loud and careening around making lunch. I notice that my kitchen and dining room are full of bags of food. Once word got out that I was in the hospital, the food fairies started delivering all kinds of goodies. The costumer from Scott's theater assembled a week's worth of meals and two scrumptious loaves of cinnamon bread. I am always surprised by how kind people can be.

During this realization, my mother-in-law plunked the baby in my arms. Everyone in the room took a breath. What did they think would happen? Would I toss her to the floor in disgust? Would I now proclaim that I was cured because I had clapped my eyes on this precious infant? Nothing dramatic happened. She was cute and sleeping. Still, she didn't feel like she had once been a part of me. I wanted to put her down and go hide in the bedroom, but was afraid about what everyone else would think. I didn't want to give them any more cause to worry or to think I was a sucky mom.

I did okay until we actually sat down for lunch. I was starving, ready to devour an entire loaf of cinnamon bread solo if I couldn't eat something substantial soon. No one takes the baby from me. She decides that she is starving, too, and I try to hold a bottle with one hand and shovel food into my own gaping maw with the other. It works about as well as expected. About halfway through, I notice that there are tears dripping onto her blanket. My biggest fear is that Scott will see this and deliver me back to Tower 4. My second biggest fear is that he won't. I hand the baby off to my dad, grab my plate, and retreat, convinced that I just can't do this mom thing, that I must lack some genetic programming that makes women love their babies.

Once sequestered in the bedroom, with its Early Tenement vibe, I start flipping through the massive wad of papers that was shoved into my hands as I was walking out of the Psych Ward doors. Most of it is about my drugs—why I should continue to take them and what sorts of side effects may creep up. My favorite is a warning that I should talk to my doctor if I have "odd or unusual dreams or thoughts." What would qualify as odd right now? Dreams that I can handle everything with my usual aplomb? I also make a mental note to call someone should I experience mouth sores, severe vomiting or diarrhea, muscle stiffness, twitching or shaking, and a painful, ongoing erection of the penis not caused by sexual arousal.

Scott pokes his head in to make sure I'm not up to anything unfortunate. Since I'm only brooding and not actively hurting myself, he gives me a kiss and goes back to the theater. His mom has the baby and my dad is doing dishes. They wanted Scott to pass on that I should stay back here for as long as I want. While I don't like being treated like a child who isn't capable of adult behavior, it is nice to not have to be responsible right now. I feel like I should be pitching in my fair share of the labor. But I can't. I know that I'll be overwhelmed by merely walking out of the bedroom. I may be able to refrain from crying during the next hour. It seems doable only if I stay very, very still, avoid my baby, and don't talk to anyone.

From my journal, July 16 (evening):

"To Do: Call about nanny tomorrow; Balance checkbook.

"Home again, home again.

"As anxious as I was to get back here, I'm terrified. I'm so scared that I can't handle this that I just want to cry.

"Everyone seems to be walking on eggshells around me—constantly checking on my mood. I don't know what to tell them half the time. I'm OK, I guess, just scared as hell.

"Part of me misses Tower 4—the relative peace, the lack of responsibility and even some of the people. It was a vacation from reality, which I needed. But like having a baby, the first step was huge. Having the time to do nothing but read was great, though, and I'll miss it.

"Scott is going to be a great dad. Right now he's walking the floor with you and making silly faces and noises—something that I never thought he'd do. Maybe it's just the sleep deprivation.

"Part of me really misses our old life, when it was just the two of us and we could do whatever we wanted to— even if it was just staring at the TV. It's not like we were party-hoppers. Having you has changed everything. I worry that we'll never be just us again, which is sad because I'll miss just hanging out with your dad.

"Back to Tower 4—what amazed me most, I think, were the transformations. I could literally watch someone put herself back together. True personalities would emerge from the emotional debris. In a way it was stunning how quickly it would happen. I don't know if it was the result of the drugs or the groups or just being in a place where it was OK to be as crazy as you wanted to.

"Toward the end—especially my last day—those faces started to look so familiar, like I'd known these people for years and we'd all just happened to be in the same hospital together. Maybe that is an effect of the drugs or, simply, spending so much emotionally charged time together. Probably it's both."

Because she is a kind woman and a nurse used to working nights, Scott's mom takes the wee-hours shift with the baby that first night. We set Maddy's car seat, which is quickly becoming the only thing she'll sleep in for any length of time, next to our guest futon, which is in the middle of the living room. For eight straight hours, Scott and I sleep like cats, curled up and oblivious to any outside noises. It is bliss.

We deal with potential perils of the next day by scheduling ourselves into a frenzy—a trip to the museum with lunch to follow if the baby's mood holds. The Knoxville Museum of Art has always been one of my favorite places to haunt. A big, white, square building dropped on the edge of a bluff that overlooks the graying skycrapers downtown, it doesn't match the rest of the city. It is perfect for the site, however, even though some of the old money in town was horrified to move into the twentieth century with such a modern building and exhibits that don't re-volve around the old masters. Knoxville is that kind of place. I find it a vaguely subversive act to embrace with reckless abandon that building and its frequently challenging shows. When I belonged to the working world, I'd pop over during particularly trying days, just to chill out among the art. It is a sanctuary.

We're there in the middle of a weekday and the place is almost empty, which turns out to be a good thing because the baby refuses to behave like a civilized human. At one point, I am pushing the stroller with one hand while holding a bottle in her mouth with the other. I keep tripping over my own feet because I'm also trying to look at the art. It's my first chance in weeks to let my brain escape into something truly beautiful. I refuse to leave just so that I can feed my child, because that would be admitting my old life is even further out of my reach, a defeat. Surrender is impossible, even though I would need to be an octopus to function well at this very moment.

At some point, my mother-in-law scoops up the baby and carries her away to parts unknown. My dad and I wander the museum in peace. We don't have much to say to each other. I know he wants to know how I am. I also know that if he asks, I'll start crying again. He must know that and, so, doesn't ask. I get the feeling that he simply wants to hug me until all of the bad stuff goes away, which is impossible.

We find Scott's mom and the baby in front of an enormous cobalt horse, part of a larger installation. Char is whispering to Maddy, describing the scene to her and explaining about both horses and colors. A knife twists in my chest. I should be doing that. It is what mothers do. Yet it never would have dawned on me to do so. My instincts are completely untrustworthy.

Rather than risk lunch, we flee back to the house, which is still full of food. My stated reason for avoiding a restaurant is that the baby seems unsettled. My real reason is that I'm starting to panic. My hands are shaking. Tears are just below the surface, ready to gush. My biggest fear is that I'll lose it in a public place and run into someone I know. Knoxville isn't big enough to avoid anyone and rumors of my demise would spread quickly.

The schedule, which had included a jaunt to the mall, is tossed in the crapper. Instead, we all lie down for naps, which the baby lets us take. By the time I wake up, my dad is doing dishes, my mother-in-law is playing with Maddy, and my husband is home from work and pondering what to do about dinner. We order barbecue from the joint down the street and gorge ourselves on smoked meats. Maddy watches us from her car-seat perch, which is on a spare dining room chair. It's like she can't believe she's related to these people who are gnawing on bones and covered in sauce.

Afterward, I have the best mom experience I had had since becoming one almost a month previous. Since Maddy's umbilical cord stump fell off while I was "away," we can finally immerse her in a tub and give her a real bath. Maddy is absolutely delighted by it, cooing and kicking. I spend a good half hour in there, watching her enjoy the water and naming all of her parts for her. Her big blue eyes never leave my face. It is miraculous. Of course, I almost drop the wet, slippery child as I'm trying to maneuver her from tub to towel, but I can forgive myself for that.

The next day, my mother-in-law leaves. She doesn't want to go, but her employers are starting to sound especially grumpy about her taking any more days off. I assure myself that the training wheels have to come off sometime. I just wish it could be after I felt less wobbly. My dad will still be around, however, for one more day. Then I'm on my own. I try to not think that far ahead because I can't breathe if I do.

The baby and I pass the day lounging on the couch, with occasional breaks for meals. My dad makes a grocery run, then we all watch really bad daytime TV. My aunt Linda, who was vacationing in the Smokies with her church youth group, drives up to our place to lay her eyes on the new family member. She plucks Maddy out of my arms and nuzzles her. Confidence flares around her like a fresh orange halo, so bright that it is almost blinding. When she leaves, I secretly feel she should take the baby with her, because she is so much more of a mother than I will ever be.

This is also the day of phone calls. The postpartum doula, Kimberly, who I met in the ER, is able to come over three afternoons per week. It's fabulously expensive, an extravagance I can't help but feel guilty about. But I give in to my weaknesses and admit that I need the help, even if it will drain our last financial cushion. My mom calls shortly thereafter, to tell me again that she told me this would happen and to volunteer to help defray some of the unforeseen costs. I take the money but feel guilty about it. She also makes noises about coming up to stay with us again, but everyone in the house, including my dad, take turns assuring her that that would be a really bad idea right now. I can barely deal with brushing my hair on a daily basis. Deflecting her passive-aggressive ego-killing rays would be beyond even Wonder Woman. A mere mortal has no chance.

Later in the day, my mother-in-law calls to let us know she's arrived safely. She also lets us know that her pictures from her first trip down are adorable. Well, the pictures of the baby are adorable. The pictures of me are, well, to put it kindly, as she says, "You could see something was wrong." When I see these snaps later, I am horrified. I look like Lurch from the Addams Family but with long, snarled brown hair and a thousand-yard stare. Most memoirists would now write, "I don't know who that woman was. It was like looking at a stranger." That's utter nonsense. I know exactly who that woman was and I know exactly where she is now. If I'm not careful, she could drop by at any time. Some days she's further away than others. And, some, she's right next door, putting on her coat to walk to my house. I have learned to live with the knowledge that she exists.

My father-in-law calls. First, he's checking to make sure that I'm still out of the pokey. He also lets us know that he's had a revelation. Since he's a second-grade teacher and off until Labor Day, he could just hop in the car, drive down from Rochester, and hang out with me for a week or two. He's also just talked to his ex-wife, who must have reported to him that we could still use some help. Scott is floored. His parents almost never voluntarily speak to each other. He's not even sure that they talked during our wedding. My madness, it seems, has forced them to bridge their differences and work together to make sure that their grandbaby has a mother. It is oddly heartwarming.

But truth be told, I don't want him to come down. I'm starting to feel stubborn. I don't want to be coddled. I am strong. I can make it on my own, just like I've done for almost everything in my adult life. Still, the idea of being completely alone in the house with this sub-ten-pound human makes my knees wobbly. I tell him I'll call him back the next day, once I've had a chance to think about it. While I have been improving, I realize the odds of full functionality returning during the next twenty-four hours is as unlikely as Tom Cruise being attacked by flying monkeys who throw tomatoes and sing "The Yellow Rose of Texas." A girl can always hope.

The day passes, as does the night. At some point during the next few days, my life takes on a curious flatness. I get up. I sit on the couch. I watch bad daytime TV and don't care about any of it, except for *Martha Stewart Living* and *Sorority Life*, which I watch with religious fervor. Nothing else makes an impression. I feed the baby. I change the baby. I watch the baby sleep. I can't seem to nap myself, no matter how I try. I make the occasional list of frighteningly easy things to accomplish. People talk to me, but it never makes much of an impression, like I'm sandwiched between two panes of thick glass. I'm in here, but nothing can get through. It is better than the continual crying, granted, but this near-vegetative state isn't all that interesting to write about. Assume that I'm planted on the couch for most of this time. Some highlights follow.

I go to see my second shrink, one who was recommended by my OB and who didn't have an appointment available before my trip to the ER. I'll still be seeing Dr. G, but to talk only about meds, since that is his specialty. When I see Dr. G, I'll also be spending time with his dog, Punch, a boxer with the sweetest personality I've ever encountered, who hangs out in the office. He's a good boy and never fails to make me feel better, no matter how poorly the day has gone. His big brown eyes offer absolution as he rests his anvil of a head on my lap. Punch is better than a priest and only makes you feel guilty if you fail to scratch behind his petal-soft ears.

My dad is going to stay with the baby until I get back from this appointment. Then he needs to hit the road to make it back to Columbus before dark. I do just fine during the twenty-minute drive to the second shrink's office, the first solo trip I've taken in weeks. It's nice to drive again and I turn up the radio, getting lost in pop songs about heartbreak and hot summers. I also do just fine during the wait to see the second shrink, flipping through a copy of *People* magazine, which I allow myself only in waiting rooms. Once I'm in her tastefully decorated room, however, the waterworks start. By the end of the session, the top half of my shirt is so wet with my own tears that I need to wring it out.

She is a godsend, the new shrink. She lets me unload all of my accumulated Mom stuff on her. I go on and on and on about how I think I'm going to fail because I can't seem to do what I've been told I had to do in order to raise a functional child. I can't sit and stare lovingly into her eyes the whole time she sucks on a bottle because the boredom makes me profoundly antsy. I can't seem to set up a bedtime routine because I'm just too tired. I don't know that I can give her all of the sensory input she needs because I don't have flash cards or know many baby songs. Because of this, my child will fail to develop and it will be all my fault. Plus, she'll hate me, because I don't have the slightest clue what I'm doing and because a lot of the time I wish she'd just shut up so that I can sleep for more than three hours at a time.

My shrink assures me that guilt about perfection and resentment for the intrusion are perfectly normal. I am not a Bad Mother for wanting to sleep. I don't have to stare into the baby's eyes every minute of every day. I have the shrink's permission to flip through a magazine if the boredom takes over during feedings. Bonding will come, but it won't be immediate. These next few weeks will probably be ugly, but I am the only one who will remember them. And they are *not* going to scar the baby for the rest of her life; nor will she hate me because of them.

My shrink is a latter-day version of the angel who visited my mother on the night I was born, patting my back and assuring me that it will all work out okay. But she's an angel that I'll get to see again and again.

Before I leave the appointment, she asks two questions. First, did I think that my depression and angst and fear would have been as bad if my baby had been a boy and I hadn't been able to project my problems with my mother onto my own daughter? And, second, when I mentioned that my father-in-law offered to come down but that I was planning to tell him not to because I am strong, she asked, "Why must you make this so hard?"

I still don't know how to answer either.

From my journal, July 23:

"Had a pediatrician visit today. All is well and you are up to 9 pounds, 8 ounces. You also got your hepatitis B vaccine—your first one. You looked so surprised when the needle went in, then you started screaming. Fortunately, a bottle calmed you right down.

"Unfortunately, next week and the following week your father goes into tech [tech is when a theatre gets a show ready to open, which includes adding lights, costumes, sound and sets, and means that those involved rarely have time to shower, much less hang out with their crazy wives], which means that he really won't be home. I'm freaking out a bit, simply because the isolation may drive me crazy again. I'm *so* scared and don't know what to do. Hopefully, a solution will present itself and soon.

"It's raining right now. A real downpour. Normally I'd find it soothing but just can't be soothed right now. The panic is rising too quickly. But I'm trying to breathe and think moment by moment. You are very cute and your daddy is coaxing you back to sleep and I am crying."

July 24:

"Today was a better day, although the morning started out a bit shakey. You were up for your 4 a.m. feeding then decided to stay up until 7 a.m. You stayed awake until about 1:30 p.m. with just a few 10-minute catnaps. We think you're going through a growth spurt We shall see.

"I also got to get out of the house today and go to Barnes and Noble. It doesn't sound like it should be a thrill but it was. I also stopped into Toys R Us and bought some puzzles to take to Tower 4. Hopefully, I'll get a chance to run up there this weekend.

"While at B&N I picked up a copy of the classic 'Madeline.' Your daddy is on the couch reading it to you. Very cute. Oh—and you turned one month old today. Whee!

"One thing I am always struck by is how in-your-body you are. When hungry, you eat like a junkie cooking up his next fix. You look almost drunk after a good feeding. When gassy, you fart with reckless abandon. And when asleep, you become like a coma victim, oblivious to the waking world. We wonder what you dream about. Giant breasts? Pinkies? Bath time? Of course, by the time you are old enough to ask, you will no longer remember."

Scott's dad, who we did ask to come down, hangs out with me for a week. I am not quite sure what we talked about, but I remember watching a lot of cable movies. At some point, I leave the baby with him and deliver the new puzzles to Tower 4. The staff looks at me like I'm insane, which isn't far from the truth, but accept my offerings. Some future loon will thank me.

Whenever Kimberly comes over, Scott's dad and I make a break for it and go shopping. Neither one of us is really predisposed to spending time at the mall, but it is something to do where there is air-conditioning. He also convinces me that I can go for a walk with the baby in her stroller. We do this one day shortly before he leaves. At the end of our street, a mere mile down the boulevard, is the main road and a great Mexican restaurant. It's a walk that I've made many, many times, even when pregnant. Now, I get about two blocks in before having to turn back. I'm covered in sweat and wobbly-kneed. When did my life get to be so sad?

Still, the knowledge that I could pack a baby in a stroller and walk around without dying is freeing, even if I can only make short jaunts at a time. After Scott's dad heads back north, I go walking every morning. The first few times I'm convinced that we are going to be run over by rogue pickups or mugged by the retirees who populate most of the street. It gets better. Without fail, Maddy spends the first fifteen minutes taking in the world, then crashes into a peaceful sleep. After a while, I can make it to the Mexican restaurant and back again. I'd stop in for a bite but always take my walks long before they're open. Even that doesn't save me from the worst of Knoxville's summer heat. It's in the eighties by the time I get back home, which is always before 10 a.m., so that I don't miss Martha Stewart. I ponder moving my walks to the mall, but the logistics of packing both the baby, her stuff, and myself in a car are overwhelming. Two years ago I navigated a rental car through Britain's B-roads using nothing but a lousy guidebook map. Now, I can't take a baby two miles up the road for shopping. Oh, how the mighty can fall.

Scott's two-week tech leaves me burning up the phone lines and calling in every last favor I can. I know that I can't handle being alone for nearly fourteen straight days without coming unglued again. I toss what little pride I have left into a small, mockable heap and beg friends to come over. And they do, which amazes me. And sometimes they also bring treats from the outside world, like falafels and turkey melts and pizzas and gossip.

Most haven't heard the story of the Psych Ward. Those few who knew about it as it was happening remained mostly mum. And each night, I tell the story again. I still have no nifty harmony worked out, but each time I launch into the litany, it makes more sense. I start developing set pieces, like the flock of doulas and Spalding Gray and Angola. I can only talk about it with colorful anecdotes, however. Talking about the shame takes much, much longer.

As long as someone else is in the house, I'm fine. When left to my own devices, however, the system breaks down. Paranoia sets in. I've been through tech at least nine dozen times and know how consuming it is, but rationality can be hard to find at 2 a.m.

From my journal, 5 August:
"The fact that Scott can't find a way to actually be at home more often must mean that there is something fundamentally wrong with me. Why would he want to be here anyway? If he feels so guilty, why can't he work on changing the situation instead of whining about how guilty he feels? His guilt is really no replacement for an actual spouse. I'm so tired and angry about always feeling like I'm being unreasonable by wanting a husband who is actually present. Why can't I find a way to get used to this. But if I were really what he wanted in a wife, he would be home more. So I must not be what he wants. Especially now."

There are, in fact, actually spots on this page where my tears made the ink run. This fit of rage and jealousy is not my finest moment in a long, long series of not-finest moments. I add to it by becoming rabidly convinced that Scott is actually having an affair. Once tech ends and he's home again with some regularity, I turn on him, hurling accusations and recriminations at the one person who hasn't wavered at all during this whole debacle. It isn't pretty. And as easy as I now find it to talk about the baby, the depression, and the aftermath, I can't give you the details on how much bitter ugliness I piled on him. I am too ashamed, even now. I don't know why he stayed.

August 8, the day that sparkles like a polished diamond:
"Yesterday, you graced us with your first real smiles. You're gonna break some hearts with that grin, kiddo. Melted mine."

I'd like to say that that was all it took and I was cured. That would be complete and utter bullshit, but it did get better. Time passed. I found ways to fill it. I walked. I sweated. During one such jaunt, the phrase "Hillbilly Gothic" came to me as I was trying to come up with the right description of my mother's family. I was next to the Presbyterian church on the corner, waiting for the light to change so that I could cross the street. The fact that I filed it away as great fodder for a writing piece proves that I was able to envision a future again, and one in which I could work. I had a strange epiphany, right there in front of the church, a realization that this strange summer was but a passing phase. And then someone cranked up a lawn mower and I lost the rest of the thought in the din. The Lord does work in mysterious ways.

I stopped writing in my journal, mostly because I didn't feel compelled to anymore. Also, the time that I would have spent writing, I spent napping. Yes, the sleep fairy was making regular rounds to the bedroom again. I had missed her, even though I've always pictured her looking like Kirstie Alley.

Rather than brood when the baby napped, I flung myself into reorganizing my life whenever I felt rested enough. I started simply, with a nebulous desire to re-arrange baby clothes so that I could always find what I was looking for. I plunked Maddy, who was snoozing in her car seat, in the middle of the nursery and got to work, filling all of the empty floor space with the con-tents of every closet and drawer. She woke up, of course, in the middle of it. When she drifted off again after a bot-tle, I went back to work. By the time Scott came home, everything was in its place and I was smirking like a self-satisfied cat.

The next day, I tackled our linen closet/medicine chest. It took a week, what with scheduling around the naps. After that, I took on the bookshelves. Scott kept coming home to stacks of books covering every flat surface in the house, with the baby and her car seat plunked in the middle of them somewhere. My eyes took on the zeal of a professional organizer. By the end of a couple of weeks, I had three diaper boxes of unwanted books to take to the used bookstore and shelves that were actually alphabetized and sorted by genre. I amazed even myself with that last feat, given that my previous strategy was simply to cram books in wherever there was an open space.

The rest of the time I filled with knitting hats, which I'd learned how to do after writing a story on local knitting groups, of which there are many in Knoxville. I couldn't devote much time to these hats before I had Maddy. All that I knew how to knit was a simple cap with a rolled brim. Folks were always asking me when I was going to do some bootees or a blankie. "I only do hats," I'd tell them, "and only sporadically."

But during my organizational phase, I found a ragged piece of knitting that needed to be finished. It was something I could do with my hands while the baby hung out with me on the couch or slept in my lap. When I ran out of yarn, I worked up the courage to lug her to my favorite yarn shop one day. The owner made the appropriate fussing noises and amused the child while I shopped for more hat yarn. It was a tiny accomplishment, but my pride was immense. A few weeks later, I picked up a book of kids' sweater patterns and started one a few days later. It wasn't nearly as hard as I'd anticipated.

* * *

From my journal, August 29:

"So it's been a while since I've written. Things have been busy—and more stable. I still have doubts—lately my biggest fear is that you're not getting enough sensory input to develop properly—but I am generally more confident.

"Some thoughts and observations:

"When you eat and it's going well, you ball up your fists under your chin and curl your toes up. Nothing has ever tasted so good.

"You love walks and are more alert than ever when we go out.

"There's some ancient intelligence living behind your eyes. And you seem so pissed off that your body won't do exactly what you want it to.

"We almost have you on a schedule where you eat a lot every four hours. Tonight may mark the end of that, given how fussy you've been, but it was nice while it lasted.

"Oh, and today marks the day when I cut my hair really short. Not sure how I feel about it yet. It makes me look a lot more like my mom, which is disturbing as hell. I may have made a grave mistake."

September 3:

"First day back to work tomorrow and your first day at day care. Last week, I couldn't wait to hand you off and have some contact with other adults. Now, though, I break into tears about leaving you in a strange place. Will they know how to play with you? Will you be scared of the unfamiliar faces and surroundings? Will you cry the whole time? If I didn't need to get out of the house so badly, I would call the whole thing off. We shall see . . ."

On that day, after dropping off Maddy at day care and shedding a few requisite tears, I made a quick stop at the Salvation Army because it was on the way back downtown. I dropped a half-dozen knitted caps and my green floral pajamas into the box. And then I went to work.

11

I make it sound so easy. Just knit a few hats, clean out a few closets, go for a few walks, et voilà, sanity. While this isn't untrue, it isn't the whole truth. But the whole truth is remarkably boring, just like most of day-to-day life is. Some days, during my forced confinement with the child, I did nothing more impressive than watch TV and read *Entertainment Weekly*. Occasionally, I would spend a whole day crying because I couldn't find a clean T-shirt and lacked the will to wash one. On those days, I did my best to get out of the house, to pack up the baby and head for any space that contained other people. On really bad days, I'd inflict myself on my friends, especially the ones who were willing to listen to me gripe and who usually had snacks in their cupboards.

I wish there were a miracle cure. I could make an astounding amount of money by marketing it. There isn't. The only way to get through it is by getting through it, by finding a good shrink or two and listening to their advice. Eventually, one of my mental-health professionals said that I was now in the same zip code as sane, and that was enough to make the struggle less of one. The advice worked for me, even though I still felt like a stranger to myself most of the time.

But I'm not sure that's a bad thing. Andrew Solomon, in his book *The Noonday Demon*, an atlas of his own depression, talks about the unseen benefits of losing your mind. "Psychiatric illness often reveals the dreadful side of someone," he writes. "It doesn't really make a whole new person. Sometimes the dreadful side is pathetic and needy and hungry, qualities that are sad but touching; sometimes the dreadful side is brutal and cruel. Illness brings to light the painful realities most people shroud in perfect darkness. Depression exaggerates character. In the long run, I think, it makes good people better; it makes bad people worse. It can destroy one's sense of proportion and give one paranoid fantasies and a false sense of helplessness; but it is also a window onto truth."

The person I was before the baby is gone, for the better, I think. It's not that I was horrid—at least, I don't think I was—but I was quick to judge others and in constant fear of being found out as a fraud. I lived my life in pursuit of perfection, because that was the only way that I felt the world would deem me worthy of its love. Now, I just don't give two shakes about making the world love me. I know who does and that it is based on who I really am, not who I want you to think I am. I spent too much time in my twenties running, denying that the past could have any influence on my present. Screw that. I'm too tired to play that game anymore, especially since striving toward being honest is so much more rewarding.

I don't mean to paint myself as a saint, one pure woman in search of authenticity who brings with her an aura of peace, calm, and beatific enlightenment. Most days, I'm happy I remember to brush my hair, much less polish my halo. I have been known to scream at Maddy, who, at almost three, is now referred to as the Diva. I have also been known to scream at the spouse, especially when I'm not feeling he understands how hard it is to be a mom, a writer, a teacher at the local college, and the chief scheduler and cook. I have been known to serve popcorn with a side of butter and salt for lunch. The Diva is not enrolled in soccer and gymnastics and swimming and ballet. She watches TV. She eats red dye and French fries and nonorganic produce, but generally not at the same time. The holier-than-thou mommy patrol, who believe in breastfeeding until college and growing their own organic flax, would be appalled. Which is fine, really, because they aren't very much fun to hang out with in the first place. I can be perfect and completely insane or good enough and sane enough. I choose the latter—but it is always a choice. I have options, but this is the best way for me to be right now.

Two years ago, the choice was harder and made on an almost hourly basis. Maddy was still in the clingy, squirmy creeper stage, where she spent every waking moment trying to crawl, walk, or chew her way into extreme peril. Sleep was fractured most nights, since she never reliably slept through the night until she was almost two. Family was so far away that free help was hard to come by. Scott's theater was struggling to make payroll, much less to provide nutty things like insurance and time off. While I can look back at individual stories I wrote with pride and firmly believe the writing helped keep me on this side of functional, the idea of working for the alternative press (or any press, really) had lost its appeal. It was time for a change. Our lives now fit us like too-small pantyhose, uncomfortable and riding up in weird places.

We decided to head north, back to the lands of our births. The single goal was to move some place near at least one of our parents. Scott dusted off his MFA and started to scour the Northeast for teaching gigs. I started to do more freelance work and fantasized about writing a book. After a few months, we found a state college in Up-state New York that wanted Scott as their technical direc-tor. Conveniently, they also had an adjunct slot open for me. The downside is that they made the decision about a month before we had to be there. It was a scramble to get houses on and off the market, packed, moved, unpacked, and settled in to. The short lead time left me with virtu-ally no day-care options once we moved. Two days a week were all I could find coverage for, which left me two days of scrambling to figure out what to do with the Diva in a town where I knew no one. Add to that the stress of teaching for the first time and finding a new shrink/gro-cery/pediatrician/coffeeklatsch and you have the perfect ingredients for a breakdown.

Which, predictably, happened. The exact start date is hard to pinpoint. I know where the end is, which is about a week after my cat died. But the beginning is hard to wrestle to the mat. I spent most of the time leading up to the move in a state of shock, wandering about our Knoxville fixer-upper and randomly throwing things into boxes. Friends held a going-away shindig, but we had to leave the party early because we had more packing to do. It took until the wee hours to load the truck. Moving day came early when we chucked the last of our stuff in and drove off.

That was the plan, anyway. What really happened is that the truck got stuck at the bottom of our driveway, where it makes a nearly right angle onto the street proper. The trailer hitch embedded itself into the soft August asphalt. Our neighbor on the other side—the one who isn't obviously crazy but does spend most of the fall practicing his bow hunting on Styrofoam deer in his backyard—crafted an elaborate series of levers and pulleys, in the hope that we could just perform a down-home truck angioplasty, popping that bad boy out of its nook. No luck. A tow truck was called, then another when the first wasn't mighty enough to do the job. Three hours later, we were on our way, $150 lighter and already frazzled.

While the men, who included Rodney, an acquaintance of an acquaintance who we'd convinced to drive the truck while we followed with a car full of baby, plants, and cats, futzed, I sat in the now-empty living room and cried. Maddy toddled around our now-empty home, and it killed me that there was no way that she would remember this place, this dumpy little house that had become a part of Scott and me. When that became too maudlin, I packed her up and went for one last drive around the city to pay it my last respects. We drove past the hospital where she was born and I went mad. We drove past the office, where I no longer belonged. We drove through the Old City, where I lost a good deal of my hearing but saw many great bands. She fell asleep. I cried and drove.

By the time we got on the road—really got on the road—I couldn't stop crying. I sobbed most of the way to Virginia, where we stopped for the night. The next morning, I cried to the New York State line while I sat in the passenger seat and knitted a belated birthday hat for a former coworker. I want to say that it was something about the scenery that made me quit crying, that there

was something ineffable about suddenly being surrounded by the Catskills and the farms that felt like
home. But I didn't really think about that until much
later. Honestly, I think I stopped crying because I suddenly realized that we would soon have to unpack the
damn truck. Nothing like the prospect of hard physical
labor to get your head on right.

The sheer busy-ness of that first week kept my mind
occupied. But once we could find things like cereal bowls
and washcloths again, I had time to dwell. I was truly
alone again for the first time in many, many months.
Scott was busy settling into his new job. I was trapped at
home with a toddler to amuse, which meant I couldn't get
out and investigate the town. All of my time was sucked
up with child care. When Maddy slept, I wrote lesson
plans. While some of the other faculty wives with kids did
their best to help, they had their own lives to worry about.
I could feel myself receding, lost in a haze of sleeplessness
and tears. I called my new insurance company to get a list
of local psychiatrists. The waiting list for a provider my
plan covered was eight weeks. And they say there's nothing wrong with our health-care system.

Fall became early winter. I hung on. It wasn't as bad
this time, which isn't to say that I was dancing a little jig
every morning, but I was more or less functional as long
as I kept my expectations low. Scott's parents came down
frequently and took some of the burden. It was a system
that was working, at least temporarily. My hope was that
I could shake it off by the time the snow started to fly.
Then my cat died.

Of our three cats, the youngest is Satan's cat, sent to
test our resolve and patience. The middle one clearly be-
longs to Scott, meaning that my lap will do in a pinch but

I am only a stand-in for when his person gets home. The oldest was clearly my cat. We'd adopted her from an Austin shelter. She was my best pal when Scott was away, when I couldn't cope with being alone. She was my only friend for the first few days I lived in Knoxville. She wasn't the best cat ever; even for a cat she was moody and frequently expressed her angst by peeing on everything of value. Still, we'd been through a lot together, this cat and I. But nothing—except, perhaps, human folly—lives forever.

I knew it was her time when we drove to the vet's on a December night, not long before Christmas. It was snowing, the first real snow we'd had. She lay in my lap the whole way, not even lifting her head to look out of the windows. I stayed with her while the vet gave her the big pink shot. And that was it. The vet would keep her body in their freezer until the ground thawed enough for us to give her a proper planting. I wailed like a banshee to the grocery, where I had to stop first to pick up a prescription for Maddy. I ran into the head of Scott's department and tried to pretend that my eyes weren't swollen and red. I failed miserably. Scott made me dinner once I got back. And we joked about how haughty my cat had been, and how sweet when it suited her. Yet, I couldn't stop crying, and I wondered if this was the beginning of the end again.

For a week, I felt as if someone had turned me inside-out and was rubbing lemon juice into my exposed innards, which seemed like an overreaction for a mere kitty. Conventional wisdom holds that such feelings be reserved for real tragedies, like tsunamis or terrorist attacks. Luckily, classes had ended and I didn't have to think about being a professional. Also luckily, more space had opened up at Maddy's new day care, which gave me some time to myself. I talked to my shrink. I took my drugs. I went out for coffee with a new friend. I cried a lot, but it got better. I still miss the silly cat, even a year later. It's something that I can cope with, though.

Again, I wish there was a magic bullet I could point to, where I could say, Do this and you'll feel better. All I can say is that you have to take it minute by sucky minute, until it doesn't suck so much. And to not be afraid to find the help you need. Don't become invisible.

History follows you, and medical records don't lie. I want to say that the past is past, that once you get through it, you are free. But this is the kind of thing that no matter how deeply you bury it, it will always find its way back to the surface after some cataclysmic event, like fossils floating up after a flood.

Shortly before Maddy's first birthday, before we left Knoxville, I found myself in the ER again. One bright summer morning I scooped up Maddy and my wallet and a grocery list. My hands were full as I slipped on my Birkenstocks. I opened the door with my elbow and hip, and started down our back steps, just like I'd done a billion times previous. What I hadn't counted on was the baby's singular desire to be on the ground, toddling about. As I was juggling list, wallet, and keys, she lurched like a rabid anaconda, which threw me off balance and down the steps. Somehow, I had the presence of mind to chuck her into the nice, soft flower beds rather than onto the patio bricks. For this, I am thankful.

I wasn't quite as kind with myself. Somehow—details remain hazy—I managed to knock over a glazed pottery flower pot. One of the shards caught me in mid-shin and cut my leg open from there to ankle. Fortunately, the Hub was home and heard the thumps and the shrieking baby. He tore out, shoeless, and scooped her up.

"Are you okay?" He had to shout to be heard over her screams and was flipping her around to check for broken bones.

I started to say that I was, but then realized that my shoe was filling up with blood. I looked down. I could see the white of my ankle bone. "Um, no," I said. "And I think I'll need a towel." Strangely, it didn't hurt.

We limped to the car, me hunched over with a folded beach towel pressed against the gash, and drove the four minutes to the ER, the same damn one that I spend so much time in. It's too bad that that hospital doesn't offer frequent flier miles. I could be on my way to Bermuda by now.

After a brief slapstick routine in front of the doors as Scott tried to figure out how to find a wheelchair, park the car, watch the screaming baby, and tend his wife simultaneously, we made it inside. Once it was made clear that I was going to drip blood all over the nice clean waiting room, I was whisked to a treatment room. Alone. Scott and the baby were taken elsewhere to make sure she hadn't been permanently maimed by her mother's act of grace and poise. She wasn't.

I, however, had to be stitched up like a Thanksgiving turkey. After repeated offers of painkillers, I finally relented when the stitching began, because that's when it started to feel like my leg was on fire. Twenty-some stitches later, I was gauzed up, cleaned up, and inspected for other injuries. When nothing physical presented itself, I was told not to move, that I had to talk to a doctor before I could go.

So I waited. Initially, I was certain that my Spalding-doppelgänger would return. Instead, I was visited by a woman MD who couldn't have been that much older than me. It's always stunning when you realize people your age are actually in positions of relative power and responsibility. Clearly, I can't be trusted to walk out of my back door, yet here was a peer who was dealing with life and death every day. Boggles the mind, it does.

"So what happened?" she asked. I explained about the flower pot and the baby-throwing.

She kept looking at me, like there was more to the story that I just wasn't sharing.

"And then we came here?" I said, hoping that she'd pick up the narrative at that point. She didn't.

"Is there anything else you want to tell me? Is everything all right at home?" It was then that I pegged to the fact that my file was in her lap, and in that file was the full four-part harmony version of my breakdown. And I realized that my injury could easily look like something self-inflicted by a person desperate to escape her life. It was then that I wished the nurses hadn't washed off all of the potting soil that had smeared on my leg. I could have pointed to it as proof.

"Oh," I said. "No. I'm fine. Really. I'm just clumsy."

"How's your mood?"

Considering that I had taken a heapin' helpin' of Vicodin, I could honestly say that it was pretty dang good, indeed. But I wasn't allowed to leave yet, not until I managed to find the right words to let her know that there was nothing sinister afoot, that I was simply not paying enough attention to where my garden accoutrements were with regard to my big sandals. It took a while and I kept expecting her to break out a bright white light, so that she could sweat a confession out of me. She didn't, and after half an hour, I was released to my husband's waiting arms.

Like I said, history follows you.

It can be subtle, of course. Friends who witnessed the whole postpartum debacle spent many, many weeks treating me like brittle, flawed glass, ready to fly apart with the slightest chilly breeze. Conversations were filled with stuttering hesitations by both parties. I didn't want to say anything that might make someone believe that I wasn't okay. I could watch friends edit words like "crazy" and "depressed" out of their speech around me. I wanted to invest in a T-shirt that proclaimed to the world that if completely going off my gourd for a few weeks hadn't broken me, no mere word would, but I could never come up with a catchy little slogan to express the idea. My friends got over it, eventually. Some of those relationships became stronger as a result, while some drifted away after the moment of crisis passed. Such is life.

My family, those who knew, at least, got over it, too. My mother was the one exception. She called daily for a while, then weekly. Each dialogue—monologue, really— became harder to bear and I was usually in tears by the end of it. If I didn't know better, I'd say her rants were designed to push every last guilt button I had left, scripted to make sure that I knew that she was completely not responsible for what happened to me because I failed to take in thirty years' worth of advice and kind mothering. That I knew that it wasn't her fault, that everything that had gone wrong could be pinned on my shit of a father. That my mother did everything she could to help when the baby was born and that I am an ungrateful daughter who deserves to be miserable. That I had a nervous breakdown just to hurt her and because I didn't let her cuddle me when I was a kid. That she grew up in the midst of dysfunction and couldn't really be blamed for what happened after that. That I was the one who should never stop going to therapy but that she was completely fine, thankyouverymuch, and didn't need to be on any meds. And on, ad infinitum. A sample:

"What did I do to make you hate me so much?"

We're on the phone again. I'd been out of the hospital for three months or so by this point. Things were stable in our house. The crying fits were infrequent and usually triggered by situations—like a baby who inexplicably decides that daytime is for sleeping and night is for playing—that could make even the strongest man weep from frustration. Even the baby routine was finding its center and we were starting to enjoy her a little. While I'd always loved her, I was just now discovering her wonderfulness. Life was improving.

"I want to know why you don't like me." Again, my mother's voice is cutting.

"I love you, Mom," I say. If given a choice, rather than have this conversation, I would have happily gone through labor for a second time. Without the epidural.

"Why won't you let me touch you? You shrink away when I try to hug you. Daughters aren't like that with their mothers. If my mom were alive, I'd hug her all the time."

And I start to explain, mentioning the baby elephant incident and how there were more tiny little betrayals and how they all worked to erode our relationship and how I don't want to talk about it and that I know she did the best she could but it wasn't enough and I'm crying and Scott keeps handing me tissues.

"But what was it specifically?" she asks. She wants a list of every hurt, every incident.

"Mom, I don't remember anymore. I wasn't taking notes." In all the ways we are different, this has always been the most glaring. I remember patterns of behavior; she remembers incidents. Because I can't cite the time and place of everything that ever happened, it doesn't count, in her eyes.

"You didn't have it so bad," she says.

She's right. No one ever touched me in anger. There was food and cable. I was never freezing. My basic needs were met. No court in the land would call it abuse or neglect. I have nothing to whine about. I am ungrateful and ashamed for not loving her enough.

"You're right, Mom."

"You need to stay in therapy," she says. And with that line I'm back to where I was, angry and tired and ashamed. I want to hurt her back, which makes me feel even more ashamed, which makes me want to hurt her more.

"I will if you will," I say. I don't mention that my shrink had recently moved me onto a once-every-three-month schedule, simply because sane and I seemed to be on speaking terms.

"I'm fine," she snaps. "You're the one with the problem."

I can't talk.

"None of this would have happened if your father didn't shut down when you were born." And we're back on track again. Story #2 unfolds like it always does. My father was a shit when I was born. I want to scream "I didn't marry him!" But I don't. The muscles in my jaw are tight, like dams holding back the force of a flood.

"I release you," she says when she's done. "I want you to go live your life without having to think about me. I won't call you. If you have something to say, you call me. I won't ask about my granddaughter. If you don't want me in your lives, I won't be. I release you."

I am a shrew who stands between my mom and my child (never mind that I've made it abundantly clear that she can visit the baby whenever she wants). I take her at her word, though. I've finally driven her away with my petty sulkiness. Despite the guilt, I am relieved.

The next week, she calls again, like nothing has changed.

The end came when I wrote about my postpartum experience for the paper. In the piece, I mentioned that my mothering models, from Hollywood stars splashed across the entertainment pages to my peers who didn't have kids to my own family, left something to be desired. Moms exist at two poles. Either you are warm and nurturing or cold and toxic. There is no in-between. You are either the Madonna or Andrea Yates. The mail I received as a result of sharing my experience was extraordinary. So many women had been through the same thing. Some were still going through it and I was able to point them to help. It is one of the few stories that I'm proud to have written, so much so that I wanted to show it to my parents. My mother called minutes after she'd read it and promised me that she would never call me again. I spent the day crying, but wasn't sure why. It was like being given everything you've ever wanted, seconds after you realized that you don't want it anymore.

There isn't a happy ending, not really. We didn't all go

on *Dr. Phil* or a Christian retreat or some such nonsense and live happily ever after. Time passed. She didn't call; nor did I. Every now and again I'd get an e-mail from her, giving me the barest updates of her life. The next summer, she and my stepfather and two stepcousins came up for a week so that she could spend time with the baby. The day they arrived I'd just gotten back from an alternative press conference where I'd just won a lovely award for the postpartum piece. My mother tried to be happy for me but her congratulations felt hollow. It was a start, at least.

Our move north, which made it impossible for her to visit with any regularity because she doesn't fly, reopened wounds. She believed that we were doing it specifically to get away from her. Still, she stayed in contact and, unasked, volunteered a little financial help. Last Christmas, we all managed to have a pleasant visit on the north Florida farm that she and my stepfather built when they retired. She can see why I want to write about what has happened and openly admits that you have to bring things into the light of day in order to see them clearly. Maddy had an amazing time with my mom's flock of chickens and ducks and dogs. My mother is finally happy, out there with her brood. You can see it, when she talks about her life, she almost glows. We will never be the best of friends. We will never whisper secrets to each other or count on never getting hurt because of some sacred mother/daughter bond. But here is where we are. I'm choosing to trust that.

A few weeks after starting this book, I took an informal poll of the friends I've made since we moved to this small city in the Catskills. Given that I was still in a self-confessional stage when we first arrived here and felt compelled to let everyone know that I had been completely crazy but was feeling much better now, most of these folks aren't in the dark about what happened. It became a great litmus test, actually. If new people failed to shun me because of my background, I figured they were good people to get to know. Your mileage, of course, may vary. I can be open about my madness because of what I do for a living, which is sit in a room and type. The image of the hermetic, melancholic writer is one that everyone enjoys. I do my best to keep up appearances for the profession.

The informal poll of my very small sample cohort went something like this: "Just because I'm curious, [name goes here], if you didn't know from the start that I have a mood disorder, would you suspect me of having one? In short, do I strike you as nuts?" Without fail, each person answered "No." They may be humoring me, of course. But I don't think so. My disorder is under control right now. My shit is together. I don't cry without good cause. I am profoundly lucky and blessed. And there are millions of women like me, mothers who have some problems now and again but who are more or less okay. We are not freaks. We are your neighbors and your friends and your family. We are responsible, reasonable adults who need to be less ashamed to admit that we struggle sometimes.

As much progress as I've made with accepting this quirk, I still can't get past one small thing. I have a daughter. In all likelihood, I've passed this on with my genes for a big pumpkin head and long fingers. That is a fact that I can't change. But I do have control over so much of what surrounds it. I can open my mouth and try to remove some of the stigma surrounding mental illness. I'll try to keep my own moods in check, if only so that she has an example of how it can be done. I know what to look for, should she ever fall into her own emotional hell. That's about all I can do. Now we just have to wait and see how this hand plays out. You just never know which cards are at the top of the deck.

In the "Things That I Never Thought I'd Do Again" Department, currently, I'm pregnant with kid number two. This time around, it's a baby of the boy variety, which has thrown me a wee bit. I'm not sure what to do with a boy. I know the basics are the same—like girls, boys like to be full, dry, and warm—but the details are a mystery. I've been warned that I should be prepared for lots of smashing of household items and a deep fascination with his wonderful penis. Beyond that, I'm at a loss. It will be a new adventure, certainly, just like it would have been had the new baby been a girl. They just insist on having their own personalities, these kids, just like they were little people or something.

What threw me most about the boy thing was the stunning realization that all of the adorable baby girl clothes in the closet will never again be worn by one of my baby girls. This baby-in-waiting, who is currently using my spleen as a conga drum, is the last baby I'll ever have. Two feels like the right number of offspring to keep track of. I will never again see the lavender Easter dress on one of my toddlers. Or that pink onesie on my three month old. My baby girl isn't a baby anymore, but those clothes remind me of when she was. Then, I just wanted to get through it, to get to this stage where she has more independence. Now that we're here, I miss the baby, the one who made all of the depression worthwhile. It's a strange nostalgia.

Now that I've done it once, I know the reward. I understand why people wax rhapsodic about having kids. I get it now, the joy that exists in watching someone grow up, in moving from babbled words to conversations about princesses and quantum physics. It's what makes those rotten moments—those screaming, kicking, grouchy days—worthwhile. And it seems like the right thing to add a sibling. It may be selfish, but I don't want my child to grow up as an only child. She needs someone else who understands at a cellular level what she means when she says, "Mom is crazy."

Of course, I am scared there will be a repeat of the postpartum depression. Terrified, in fact. But a few things work in my favor. I've done it once and can do it again. Now that I know that it's a likely hazard, I can prepare by calling in every last favor that I can. As a writer/mom friend put it, it's like jumping into the East River in April. I know I'll survive, but it probably won't be pleasant. The rewards outweigh the risks. Sometimes, you have to jump. If you're lucky, someone will stand by with a warm towel.

Yes, my kids will think I'm crazy. That's the right of kids. It's what they do when not shoving the cat into the dryer or marking the walls with impressionist crayon art. This book will give them plenty of fodder for future arguments, for which they'll neglect to thank me. Perhaps they'll be pissed that I made their eventual rebellion too easy. All I can do is make sure that mine is a generic-grade of crazy like, "Hey, remember that time Mom left the bag of innards in the Thanksgiving turkey" rather than the "Hey, remember that time Mom hanged herself from the basement rafters" sort. I owe them this.

I had another epiphany last summer. The Hub, the Diva, and I were on our way back from visiting old college friends who now live on a tidal island in Maine. It was a good trip, despite a day of rain, and we all had a good time poking at sea critters and burying our feet in sand. Kites were flown. All our kids played with a half-dozen fresh lobsters, then fled the house when we tossed the crustaceans in the pot of boiling water. A good time was had by all, except the lobsters.

The drive back was as miserable as the weekend was wonderful. Traffic was hopelessly dense and surly. Three separate accidents resulted in multihour delays. By the time we hit the Berkshires, Maddy came completely unglued. She had had enough of being trapped in her car seat. As we crossed into New York State, she finally gave in to the reality that no amount of screaming would change her situation. She gave us one last look of utter disdain, then popped her thumb into her mouth, rubbed her blankie against her cheek, and drifted into a blissful sleep.

Miraculously, the traffic cleared shortly thereafter. We drove into the sunset, which was nicely framed by the eastern edge of the Catskills, which are really just one of the northern hunks of the Appalachians. Quietly, as a Scott Miller CD played, some neglected part of my subconscious whispered, *This is where I belong. Here. In these mountains, where you can get lost in a holler and never see a straight horizon.* The ocean is untrustworthy and changeable. Wide-open spaces without natural features to break up the monotony give me the willies. Mountains, however, will always keep you safe. They are constant and true, like a loyal dog. You just have to learn how to meet them on your own terms.

Acknowledgments

It takes a village to write a book—and I'd like to take a minute to send some thanks to mine:

To Robert Faires, my first editor ever, who gave me encouragement when I didn't even deserve it and whose microscopic comments crabbed in my margins always made my work better.

To Coury, Jesse, Joe T., Ian, and the rest of the boys for letting a girl join the club

To Elizabeth Kaplan, my agent, for taking on this project and actually selling the dang thing.

To Scott Miller, for all of the beer and sympathy.

To Emily Farmer, for her magical red pen.

To Bob Tebay, Jim Miracle, and Pam Brust for providing Parkersburg leads.

To my parents, my aunts, my cousins, and all of the extended family. I hope you aren't too unhappy with what I've made.

To the Bagbys, for being the best neighbors/friends/coworkers a family can have and, additionally, for the pies and barbecue.

Most importantly, to my husband, for being who he is, and my children. I love you.

* * *

If you or someone you know is struggling with mental illness, do not suffer in silence. Contact your local emergency services provider or the National Alliance on Mental Illness at 1-800-950-NAMI (6264).

About the Author

ADRIENNE MARTINI has been a theater technician, apprentice massage therapist, bookstore bookkeeper, and pizza-joint waitress while picking up degrees in both theater and journalism. She has written theater reviews and features for the *Austin Chronicle*, blurbs about tofurkey and bottled water for *Cooking Light*, and knitting summer camp for *Interweave Knits*. She is a former editor for Knoxville, Tennessee's *Metro Pulse* and recently won an Association of Alternative Newsweeklies (AAN) award for feature writing. During the day, she fields freelance gigs and crams knowledge into the heads of college students in Upstate New York. At all hours, she is mom to Maddy and Cory, and wife to Scott.